# HEIRLOOM
## BEANS

# HEIRLOOM BEANS

*Great Recipes for Dips and Spreads, Soups and Stews, Salads and Salsas, and Much More from*

## Rancho Gordo

**STEVE SANDO** *and* **VANESSA BARRINGTON**

*Photographs by* **SARA REMINGTON**    *Foreword by* **THOMAS KELLER**


**CHRONICLE BOOKS**
SAN FRANCISCO

BRIDGEWATER, N.J. 08807

## DEDICATION

*This book is dedicated to anyone who has ever put a seed in the ground and enjoyed the miracle that follows.*

Text copyright © 2008 by Steve Sando and Vanessa Barrington.
Foreword copyright © 2008 by Thomas Keller
Photographs copyright © 2008 by Sara Remington.

Library of Congress Cataloging-in-Publication Data available.

ISBN 978-0-8118-6069-7

Manufactured in China.

Prop styling by Carrie Brown
Food styling by Carrie Brown and Vanessa Barrington
Designed by Leone Design, Tony Leone

10 9 8 7 6 5 4

Chronicle Books LLC
680 Second Street
San Francisco, California 94107

www.chroniclebooks.com

# CONTENTS

# FOREWORD

**I HAVE ALWAYS LOVED BEANS.** I remember eating navy bean soup as a child … it was one of my favorite dishes even when it was not homemade and came out of a can. As I grew older and my palate matured, cassoulet became another favorite winter dish enjoyed with family and close friends. These food experiences bring me great comfort, as their flavors and textures are inextricably linked to memories of kinship and joyful occasions in my life.

It therefore comes as no surprise that we feature many varieties of beans on our menu. They are one of those comfort foods that evoke a sense of warmth and nostalgia, as well as a sense of wonder within us. If you have ever had the good fortune of plucking a fresh pod of fava beans and splitting it in the palm of your hand, you will be amazed at what you will discover: a row of softly glistening plump green beans, lined up like little soldiers and nestled in a cottony surrounding. It is as if Mother Nature took such a personal interest that she then carefully enveloped each bean to protect them from harm. At The French Laundry, we painstakingly shell each fava bean by hand. It is quite labor intensive but I assure you, worth every effort. Once peeled, they are cooked quickly to retain the mildly nutty, buttery, and creamy flavors they have become known for. They are my favorite harbinger of spring.

People often ask me what I believe the foundation of good cooking is. Along with flawless technique, certainly the use of high-quality ingredients at the peak of their flavor is foremost. That is the main reason why we carefully nurture our relationship with our purveyors. It is a reciprocal connection—they provide us with the finest crops available; and as cooks, we in return treat them with respect and showcase them in our dishes in the best possible way. I recall when Steve Sando delivered his first batch of beans to the restaurant and how our cooks gathered around to appraise them with curiosity. The energy and pride he exuded made us eager to cook and experiment with them right away.

Steve and I first met at our local farmers' market in Yountville, California, several years ago. What struck me about him then were his earnestness and his knowledge about heirloom beans—and of course the eye-catching, multicolored array he had on display. Because he sells his beans "new" (meaning they are harvested and dried within a year and then sold to the public), they have the most consistent quality I have ever come across. The longer beans are stored, the longer the cooking time needed for them to soften. Less cooking time means their delicate flavors are preserved and that the beans also retain their shape when cooked. Because of these wonderful characteristics, we keep several types of Rancho Gordo beans on hand at all times. At The French Laundry, we have four types of heirloom beans from Steve that we use often: black nightfall, Anasazi, *cellini runner*, and marrow beans. Our sister restaurant Per Se in New York also utilizes them frequently, as do our casual restaurants Bouchon in Yountville and Las Vegas.

Rancho Gordo has made such an impact that it has followed many chefs who have left our kitchens and who now run their own. For example, our former chef de cuisine Eric Ziebold who went on to head CityZen in Washington D.C., as well as a previous sous chef Ryan Fancher who is now at El Dorado Kitchen in Sonoma, proudly serve Rancho Gordo beans. Steve takes great pride in growing the best he can, in the best possible way he can. His heirloom beans are vastly different from what we have been accustomed to in the past, and people detect a big difference in flavor and texture once they have tried them. His efforts in cultivating these rare and obscure varieties have helped spark renewed interest within food circles.

When Steve approached me to write the foreword for his book, I thought of how beans have played a prominent role in the development of the human race. It also made me remember what I read in Ken Albala's *A History of Beans*, which mentioned that the birth of civilization thousands of years ago can be attributed to beans. They were one of the first domesticated plants and provided much-needed nutrients to the community when hunters came back empty-handed. The fact that beans have endured and played a great role in human evolution is a testament to their resilience and importance.

Whole countries and societies have sustained themselves on beans for centuries. For example, soybeans are considered one of the five "ancient grains" in China. The Chinese have found ways to use them in many ways—such as tofu, noodles, soy sauce—even soybean oil. In India, they have relied on various types of lentils and beans for nourishment, as they are one of the most complete sources of protein for their vegetarian diet.

Beans have sadly not reached the same fervor and acceptance in the United States, as for example, other staples like corn or potatoes, which I find unfortunate. This is why I give my support to Steve and his pursuit of bringing heirloom beans to the fore. His efforts make me feel hopeful on several levels: 1) that his work will help beans find the rightful niche in our culture that they deserve; 2) that on an agricultural level, he will continue to generate more attention to the importance of sustainable farming practices in our country; and finally, 3) that after reading *Heirloom Beans*, his readers will come away with an understanding of why we are committed to helping him spread the word and why we give Rancho Gordo beans a place of honor at our restaurants.

—**Thomas Keller**, *The French Laundry*

# WELCOME TO RANCHO GORDO

*"Are these beans vegetarian?"*

*I thought I must have misunderstood the question and asked the young woman what she had said. "Vegetarian! Are these beans vegetarian?" She roundly slapped several packages of my dried heirloom beans as if that would help me understand what she was asking.*

*"Do you mean organic?" I asked. My middle-aged brain makes funny leaps at times and I could see saying vegetarian when I meant organic. After all, these were uncooked dried beans. Did she think we went to the trouble of dipping the beans in beef bouillon before we dried them?*

*Clearly she was frustrated with me. "No meat. Vegetarian!"*

*"Yes," I gently assured her. "The beans are vegetarian."*

**WELCOME TO MY WORLD!** I'll try not to climb on my soapbox, but now and then you may find me wondering aloud how we got to a place where people think that beans might have meat in them. Or how we let these heirloom beans slip through our hands for so many generations. Although food politics is beyond the scope of this book, I hope we can begin discussing our collective culinary heritage here in the Americas—how to preserve it and how to eat it. My passion is for food that is indigenous to the New World. It's interesting because it's our own collective history and yet we know little about it. In these times of borders made of anger and cement, it's nice to consider our world in relation to our neighbors', and focus on the things we have in common rather than our differences. Instead of inventing new food traditions or attempting to copy Europe's verbatim, I'm more interested in looking at the ones we have, which perhaps we've neglected or ignored. What are the foods that have been cultivated here since long before Columbus arrived? Do they grow better here? Are they easier on the land? Do they use less water? How do indigenous foods combine with foods from other parts of the world? I find the whole subject fascinating, and for me the most interesting and neglected indigenous food is the common bean, *Phaseolus vulgaris*. Of course, there's nothing common about it, and some of us are spending our lives growing, harvesting, eating, and marketing the heirloom varieties that are so attractive in every sense.

I came to love beans in a roundabout fashion. One August afternoon in my town of Napa, I was shopping for a dinner party and decided to buy some tomatoes. I was at an upscale grocery store so you'd think I was in good hands, but the selection of tomatoes was sad and ugly. Instead of big, juicy beefsteaks or even ripe salad tomatoes, they were anemic, pink hothouse tomatoes from Holland. Here I was in one of the world's most magnificent agricultural regions, and I was forced to buy tasteless Dutch tomatoes. I started collecting seeds, and the following year I tried growing tomatoes for myself. Luckily, it was one of "those years" when any fool could grow good tomatoes. My bounty was beyond belief. I erroneously felt that I was talented and decided to grow professionally. I became a specialty boutique grower of really wonderful tomatoes.

All was well and good, but what could I sell while the tomatoes ripened? I called up a bean farmer I had heard about and the rest is history. I quickly learned I'm not a particularly gifted farmer, and my initial success had much to do with luck and pluck. I decided to leave the major production to the professionals, while I searched the Americas for interesting and rare beans to bring back to Napa to test on my small plot. The yield from my successful beans in Napa became seed for the growers, and I now get to be a gentleman farmer and, I hope, save some endangered beans.

My background has been geared to anything but agriculture. I grew up in the San Francisco Bay Area and started traveling as soon as I could. Instead of spending my entire senior year of high school at a desk, I decided it would be better to travel to India. The late 1970s were a different era, and it just made sense to me and, oddly, to my parents as well. I came home for a few years, then soon found myself living in London, followed by stints in Italy and Los Angeles, and finally settling back home in the Bay Area. Food was a constant interest. So were music, cocktails, and discovering what it meant to be an American. Friends are still a little surprised when we catch up and they discover my main interest is in agriculture and food politics in general, and beans in particular.

But why bother with heirloom beans? Industrial agriculture produces kidneys, great northerns, and limas that are pennies a pound. Thousands of acres in the United States, Canada, and Mexico are dedicated to growing them. The problem is, in general, they're boring. They taste like next to nothing, and you're probably going to have to spend a lot of money to make them palatable. If you purchased them in an average supermarket, chances are it's been a few years since the beans were harvested, and it's anyone's guess how long they're going to take to cook. Each variety of heirloom has its own unique flavor or texture, or both, and needs only a few aromatic vegetables or herbs to flavor the pot. I'm an omnivore, but I generally prefer to cook my heirloom beans vegetarian. Because the yields of heirloom beans are lower than bland hybrid varieties and they're harder to grow, most producers of heirlooms tend to be small artisan growers that are part of a shorter supply chain, meaning your beans are likely, although not guaranteed, to be fresher.

Beans are romantic. Take a handful of brightly colored heirlooms and put them in your pocket. Travel to Idaho or Istanbul and plant them. At first, you'll get the beautiful flowers (which are edible, by the way), followed by string beans, then shelling beans, and, finally, dry beans. You can eat some of the harvest during all of these stages, but be sure to keep some of your bounty as seed stock. This way you can collect another handful and repeat the process again the following year, in the same place or across the globe. I find this incredibly romantic.

As the heirloom beans grow, they are much like any bean. The young white beans rest snugly in a protective pod, usually green. At the end of the season, when the growing stops, the farmer cuts off the water and the plants die. The beans, suspecting the end is near, turn all kinds of fantastic colors as the pods become dry and brittle. I imagine this is nature's way of saying, "Save me! Look! I'm pretty!" Yelling this out loud has never worked for me, but as you can see from the photos of the dry beans in this book, the beans are right. If you've been looking at dried kidneys, lentils, and garbanzos your whole life, you might be a little overwhelmed at what you've been missing. I still am each time I come across a new variety.

Beans are easy to grow and have few natural enemies. Farmers often grow beans and other legumes in empty fields to keep the nitrogen in the soil from leaching away, turning the entire crop into the soil at the end of the season and treating it as "green manure" or fertilizer. Fresh organic matter is key for healthy soil development, and legumes are often the first choice, whether the beans are a food crop or not.

Every week there seems to be a new medical study showing the benefits of eating beans. One week it's black beans, and the next it's red. The truth is all beans are superfoods—loaded with protein and devoid of cholesterol. After six months of eating about half a cup a day (on average), my bad cholesterol went down while the good went up. The high fiber in beans means a slow rise in blood sugar levels after eating, making them a smart choice for people with diabetes and hypoglycemia. Beans are also high in iron and vitamins A and B, and have as much calcium as milk. Your doctor can tell you what the potassium, phosphorous, and zinc in beans can do for you. I'm just glad the nutrients are there, whatever they are.

So heirloom beans are romantic, beautiful, and actually good for the soil and your body. What's not to like? The reality is that if they tasted ordinary, none of this would much matter to me. I'm happy to eat healthy food, but if it tastes like dirt clods and used shoestrings, there's not much point. The real magic of these beans is the flavor—and not just the flavor of the beans. You'll hear me go on about "pot liquor"—which is nothing more than simple bean broth—but to a bean aficionado, it's just as important as the beans. Some beans have a thick skin and give little personality to the broth; others almost produce a soup along with the beans. The beans themselves are as varied as their markings, and it's a good idea to keep notes on which beans knock your socks off and their individual characteristics. Some are creamy and

soft, some are meaty, some are dense, and some are as light as the wings of a butterfly. Until you've had a good, fresh heirloom bean, it's hard to imagine what I'm talking about, but once you've tried a Good Mother Stallard or some *rosa de castilla*, for example, you won't be satisfied with boring supermarket beans again.

My quest for interesting food was really born out of frustration in the kitchen. At first, I thought exploring these heirloom varieties would only be of interest to me. It's been a nice surprise to find so many other home cooks and professionals interested in these beans as well. Being introduced to Vanessa Barrington, who created many of these recipes, was a bit of good luck. I think she takes the bean from being a specialty food item to a key component in our everyday cooking.

—Steve Sando

# ABOUT
## THE RECIPES

**I'VE HEARD STEVE TELL PEOPLE** to cook his beans as simply as possible because "they don't really need our help." And it's true: heirloom beans have so much inherent character and the different beans are so varied in texture, color, and flavor that they are perfectly delicious on their own. But then, I'd remind him that we were writing a cookbook! Like all great ingredients, the beans are inspiring, and once you start cooking and eating them, it's nearly impossible to ignore the temptation to create new dishes.

To develop recipes for this book, I would start by simply cooking each new variety. More often than not, as the beans simmered on the stove, the aromatic steam wafting from the pot would conjure up in my mind a fully developed gustatory snapshot of a finished dish. It was almost as if the beans were telling me what they wanted to become. Of course this didn't happen entirely without context. The weather at that moment, the seasonal produce in the markets, and my mood each had a hand in the process. Short-season produce like asparagus, green garlic, squash blossoms, corn, tomatoes, and basil all found their way into the recipes in this book.

Many of the recipes in this book were developed specifically for this project. Others are Rancho Gordo classics or recipes contributed by some of the many chefs that serve Rancho Gordo beans to their restaurant customers. It was as fun to see how other cooks' culinary inspirations played out on the plate as it was to develop new recipes for the beans.

While working on this book an unexpected thing happened: My eating habits changed. I have always loved beans, but, like most people, rarely cooked dried beans. It always seemed like too much time, trouble, planning, or all three. Through cooking countless pounds of beans, I discovered that delicious, healthful, economical, ecological, and versatile beans could easily be a central part of my diet. With little planning or effort, a pot of beans becomes the center of a meal. The leftovers then become the building blocks for countless other dishes—creating a whole new way of eating. Beans now have a regular place at my table, and hopefully will find their place at yours as well.

—**Vanessa Barrington**

# HEIRLOOM BEAN VARIETIES

*There are actually several families of New World beans. I'm sharing with you some of my favorites. This list barely scratches the surface, but is a good place to start. These are some of the beans I love and use in this book, and think you should try. That's all.*

**Anasazi Beans** *(Phaseolus vulgaris)*
Anasazis are a classic bean of the U.S. Southwest with beautiful markings. They are somewhere between a pinto and a kidney. They hold their shape but have none of the gumminess of a plain kidney.

**Appaloosa Beans** *(Phaseolus vulgaris)*
There are at least two beans that I know of called Appaloosa. My favorite is the one from New Mexico, which is like a softer version of the Anasazi. The other, less common variety is small and dense.

**Black Beans** *(Phaseolus vulgaris)*
Also known as turtle beans. There are hundreds of heirloom varieties of black beans, some tiny and others quite big. All tend to have a thick black skin and a creamy white interior.

**Black Calypso Beans** *(Phaseolus vulgaris)*
Also known as orca or yin/yang beans. Black calypso is an incredibly pretty, medium-sized white bean with black splotches. The texture and flavor are similar to a russet potato. There's a finite window when the bean is whole during cooking, before it starts to crumble and fall apart. It's no less delicious, but maybe a little less practical.

**Black Calypso Beans** *(Phaseolus vulgaris)*

**Black Valentine Beans** *(Phaseolus vulgaris)*

### Black Valentine Beans *(Phaseolus vulgaris)*

When raw, black valentines have a beautiful black matte color that makes them look like polished rocks. The black fades to gray when the beans are cooked. The flavor and texture are closer to a kidney bean than a traditional black turtle bean.

### Black Nightfall Beans *(Phaseolus vulgaris)*

The small dense beans have an almost piney, herbaceous flavor. Their texture can be a little grainy. I use them mostly as a side dish, cooked with a little rosemary and topped with some grated, dry cheese.

### Borlotti Beans *(Phaseolus vulgaris)*

The cranberry bean originated in Colombia as the *cargamanto* but its velvety texture and rich bean broth made it an ideal candidate for exportation. The Italians bred the bean to suit their tastes and *borlotti* tend to have the same flavor of other cranberry beans but they have a thicker skin, making them ideal for dishes like pasta e fagioli.

### Cannellini Beans *(Phaseolus vulgaris)*

Cannellinis are a small white bush bean developed by the Italians.

### *Cellini* Beans *(Phaseolus cocoentus)*

*Cellini* are a medium to large runner bean with a slightly thicker skin than the more common runner cannellini. Because the beans hold their shape, they're ideal for salads and composed dishes.

### Christmas Lima Beans *(Phaseolus lunatus)*

Also known as chestnut lima beans. These beautifully marked, large limas have a distinct chestnut flavor. They're ideal as a side dish, and they're often paired with sautéed wild mushrooms.

### Cranberry Beans *(Phaseolus vulgaris)*

Originally from Colombia, the cranberry bean family has traveled far and wide and yet has retained its distinct markings and creamy, almost velvety texture. Among the cranberry beans are *borlotti*, tongues of fire, French horticulture, October, *cargamanto*, and wren's egg. These beans tend to age faster than other varieties, which makes their skins darker, and they can take longer to cook, so you'll want to use them within a year or so of harvesting.

*Cellini* Beans *(Phaseolus cocoentus)*

Christmas Lima Beans *(Phaseolus lunatus)*

Cranberry Beans *(Phaseolus vulgaris)*

### European Soldier Beans (*Phaseolus vulgaris*)

Also known as soldier beans. The markings are said to represent the epaulets on a European soldier's uniform. They have an almost potatolike flavor and are traditionally used in baked beans in certain regions of the eastern United States.

### Eye of the Goat Beans (*Phaseolus vulgaris*)

Also known as *ojo de cabra* or goat's eye beans. When raw, the beans look like their namesake. The really great thing about them is their rich flavor and meaty texture. You can use them in any chili dish, but my preferred manner of serving them is just with grated raw onion and a squeeze of lime juice.

### Eye of the Tiger Beans (*Phaseolus vulgaris*)

Also known as *ojo de tigre*, tiger's eye, or *pepa de zapallo* beans. The orange and brown markings on these beans from Argentina make them one of the most appealing-looking beans. They tend to fall apart as soon as they're cooked, so I think they're best saved for serving as a refried bean.

### Flageolet Beans (*Phaseolus vulgaris*)

When raw, flageolets have a pretty, celadon green color. As they cook, they manage to stay whole and get creamier and creamier. The cooking liquid is unspectacular, but the beans' texture more than makes up for it. Traditional pairings include roasted tomatoes or lamb.

### *Flor de Junio* and *Flor de Mayo* Beans (*Phaseolus vulgaris*)

These beans, "June flower" and "May flower," can be used interchangeably. They are pretty, mottled brown beans with a somewhat dense texture, and yet they're also creamy. They age quickly, so make sure you buy fresh beans with a light color. Regionally, you'll find them in the Mexican state of Michoacán.

### Florida Butter Beans (*Phaseolus lunatus*)

Also known as calico pole beans. Outside the Deep South of the United States, the term "butter bean" is confusing. It means that the beans are to be buttered, not that they have a buttery flavor. It also refers only to baby lima beans, which are normally served as a fresh vegetable. Of course, there are exceptions, and the Florida butter bean is one of them.

**Wren's Egg** (*Phaseolus vulgaris*)

**Borlotti Beans** (*Phaseolus vulgaris*)

### Good Mother Stallard Beans *(Phaseolus vulgaris)*

I don't have a favorite bean, but given the choice, this is one of the first beans I'll reach for in the pantry. They plump up into a nice brown bean, and their pot liquor is almost like free soup. This is one of those beans that doesn't need a lot of adornment and is best made with just some onion and garlic.

### Jacob's Cattle Beans *(Phaseolus vulgaris)*

This is another classic bean of the northeastern United States, often seen in baked beans. It has the texture of new potatoes. I once used this in a cassoulet, and it was much better than flageolet beans.

### Marrow Beans *(Phaseolus vulgaris)*

These small white beans are mild, but they soak up whatever you cook with them, even if it's a simple aromatic vegetable sauté or a ham hock. When I first cooked with marrow beans, I found them somewhat lackluster compared with the more dramatic-tasting white beans, but they've become a favorite.

### *Mayacoba* Beans *(Phaseolus vulgaris)*

Also known as *canario, mayocoba, peruano,* or yellow beans. Originally from Peru, these beans are the most likely bean you'll be served in many parts of Mexico, especially the state of Jalisco. They have a thin skin and meaty interior, making them the opposite of most beans. When cooked with celery, carrot, and onion, they have an almost comfort-food flavor. Their thin skin makes them an ideal refried bean.

### Pinto Beans *(Phaseolus vulgaris)*

Despite being as common as a cold, pintos are really a delightful bean. There are modern hybrids that produce better than the old varieties, but it's a type of bean that has been around for years. Look for rattlesnake beans for a twist on this old favorite.

### Red Nightfall Beans *(Phaseolus vulgaris)*

Also known as mayflower beans (not to be confused with *flor de mayo,* a different bean). These small tan beans with red markings look almost as if someone has hand-painted their skins. When cooked, they stay whole and then tend to melt in your mouth. These beans don't age well, so try to consume them within a year or two of harvesting.

**Eye of the Tiger Beans** *(Phaseolus vulgaris)*  **Good Mother Stallard Beans** *(Phaseolus vulgaris)*  **Rio Zape Beans** *(Phaseolus vulgaris)*

### Rio Zape Beans *(Phaseolus vulgaris)*

Also known as Rio Zappe or Hopi string beans. These dark purple beans have black marks. Many people grow them for use as a string bean, but I think they really come into their own as dried beans. Their flavor is almost like pintos but with a hint of coffee and chocolate. Being so rich, they're best eaten on their own or as a side dish.

### *Rosa de Castilla* Beans *(Phaseolus vulgaris)*

You'll find this variety mostly in the state of Michoacán in Mexico. They have beautiful pink and white markings. The flavor is somewhat like *flor de mayo*, but the texture is lighter and creamier. These beans are hard to find but worth the bother of looking for them.

### Runner Cannellini Beans *(Phaseolus coccinus)*

Also known as white runner, Italian butter, or *ayacote blanco* beans. Chefs have known about these beans for years, but now many cooks seem to be choosing runner cannellini. Unlike the more common cannellini, which is a bush bean, the runner cannellini produces a large, buttery bean that needs little adornment when cooked. Most likely bred in Italy, they originated in Oaxaca, Mexico.

### Santa Maria *Pinquito* Beans *(Phaseolus vulgaris)*

Also known as pink beans or Santa Maria pinks. These beans most likely came to Santa Maria, California, with the migrant citrus workers from Mexico, but now, along with tri-tip barbecues, they're part of the local tradition. The beans are small and dense and can handle long, slow cooking without falling apart.

### Scarlet Runner Beans *(Phaseolus coccinus)*

Also known as *ayacote*. Some experts believe that scarlet runner beans were among the first domesticated crops in Mesoamerica. Originating in Oaxaca, they've traveled all over the world and now are probably most popular in England, where they are grown for their pretty lipstick-colored flowers (which are edible) and are sometimes eaten as a fresh shelling bean. Of course, I think they're best as a dried bean, served with either wild mushrooms or a rich chile sauce.

### Swedish Brown Beans

A small brown, round bean that makes a quick and delicious soup that tastes somewhat like baked beans, without all the bother.

**Runner Cannellini Beans** *(Phaseolus coccinus)*

**Red Appaloosa Beans** *(Phaseolus vulgaris)*

**Black Nightfall Beans** *(Phaseolus vulgaris)*

### Tepary Beans *(Phaseolus acutifolius)*

Teparies are a wonderful drought-tolerant crop, and the beans are higher in protein and fiber than most other beans. There are dozens of varieties, but the most common is the brown tepary. Despite their small size, they still require slow, even cooking, like other beans. The cooked bean has a slightly sweet taste.

### Vallarta Beans *(Phaseolus vulgaris)*

This very dense, soft yellow bean is almost too rich to eat by itself and is best as an ingredient in a larger dish. I've seen the beans puréed and used as a filling in ravioli, but most often they seem to be paired with a hearty green like spinach, kale, or chard.

### Vaquero Beans *(Phaseolus vulgaris)*

These black and white beans hold their shape when cooked, but their soft texture makes them feel somewhat luxurious. I've heard them described as a cross between an Anasazi and a pinto, which makes some sense. I've seen vaquero beans marked as orca beans, which makes no sense as there's already an orca bean and the markings on vaqueros look more like a horse than a whale.

### Yellow Eye Beans *(Phaseolus vulgaris)*

These white beans with yellow marks are a ham hock's best friend. Their chowdery texture absorbs the pork flavors. They're also delicious without pork.

### Yellow Indian Woman Beans *(Phaseolus vulgaris)*

Also known as Montana yellow beans. These small yellow beans have a rich, creamy interior, making them almost more like a black turtle bean than anything else. I always recommend them for chilis and stews, but as with most good heirlooms, a simple bowl of these beans alone makes a great meal.

**Vallarta Beans** *(Phaseolus vulgaris)*    **Yellow Eye Beans** *(Phaseolus vulgaris)*

# BASIC COOKING TECHNIQUES FOR A
# SIMPLE
# POT OF BEANS

*There isn't one single best method of cooking beans. When you're in a hurry, you may want to use a pressure cooker. On a leisurely, rainy Sunday, you might want to put a clay pot full of beans in the fireplace. At the most basic, you want to simmer the pot until the beans are soft. Soaking can speed up the process, and vegetables or broth will make the beans more flavorful. It's really that simple.*

## Soaking the Beans

Normally on a bean-cooking day (which happens two or three times a week at Rancho Gordo), I put the beans to soak in the morning, after rinsing them in lots of cool water and checking them for small bits of debris. I cover the beans with about 1 inch of cold water.

You will hear that changing the soaking water cuts down on the flatulence factor of beans. For every person that tells you this, there is another, normally a food scientist, who will declare it to be false, or the results negligible. I've cooked a good number of pots, and I can tell you from my own experience it makes no difference. The only thing you can do to prevent gas is to eat beans more often, and your body will learn how to digest them. If you haven't had beans in a while or you eat a very low-fiber diet, I don't recommend you begin with a big bowl of beans. Start slowly, and you won't have a problem.

Others insist that beans don't need to be soaked at all. The entire nation of Mexico, for example. Although I prefer to eat in Mexico over almost anyplace else in the world, I have done side-by-side comparisons and found that beans soaked in water for 2 to 6 hours have a better texture and cook more evenly. But if you hate the idea of soaking, skip this step.

Another trick is called the quick-soak method. Advocates of this technique pour hot water over the beans and let them soak for about 1 hour, then pour off the water, add new water, and start cooking. This sounds scientific, but when you think about it, soaking in hot water is virtually cooking, so why not just start cooking? Obviously I'm no fan of this method, but you are bound to meet some bean cookers who are adamant about it. It's best just to nod in agreement and then go ahead and do what you want.

## Flavoring the Beans

Heirloom varieties don't need a lot of fussing if they are used fresh, which I'd define as within two years of harvesting. You can cook them with a ham bone or chicken broth, or, as I prefer, simply with a few savory vegetables like onions and garlic. Another option is a classic mirepoix, a mix of finely diced onion, celery, and carrot, sautéed in some kind of fat, often olive oil. A crushed clove of garlic doesn't hurt. If cooking Mexican or Southwestern, I sauté onion and garlic in mild bacon drippings or even freshly rendered lard (page 110). I think flavoring with a mirepoix is the best way to cook a good bean. I love fussing in the kitchen, but this is all you need.

Keep in mind that salt, acids, and sugars can negatively affect the beans as they cook. So don't add these flavorings until after the beans are soft. This includes molasses in baked beans.

If you're stuck with old, standard supermarket beans, cooking them with a ham hock and chicken broth might be a good idea, but heirloom varieties taste as good as they look and don't need a lot of help. To save cleanup time later, I sauté the vegetables in the same pot I use to cook the beans. Once the vegetables are soft, it's time to move on to the next step.

## Cooking the Beans

Pour the beans and their soaking water into a large pot. The beans will have expanded, so make sure they are still covered by about an inch of liquid. If you haven't cooked the mirepoix in the pot, add it now and give a good stir. Raise the heat to medium-high and bring to a hard boil.

Keep the beans at a boil for about 5 minutes and then reduce the heat to a gentle simmer. I like to see how low the heat can go and still produce the occasional simmering bubble. If too much heat is escaping, cover the pot. If the simmer turns into a boil, remove the lid or set it ajar. Allow the beans to cook. This can take 1 hour or even 3 to 4 hours, depending on the age of your beans. When the beans are almost ready, the aroma will be heady. They will smell not so much like the vegetables you've cooked with them but like the beans themselves. At this point, add salt. Go easy as it takes a while for the beans to absorb the salt. For my taste, I find a scant 2 teaspoons salt per pot, made with 1 pound dried beans, is ideal, but this is very subjective. If you want to add tomatoes or another acidic ingredient like lime or vinegar, wait until the beans are cooked through.

If the liquid in the pot starts to get low, you can add more water. Mexican cooks will tell you that cold water hardens the skins and that you must add hot water to keep the beans soft. I keep a pitcher of room-temperature water nearby, and so far the beans I've cooked have never suffered from tough skins.

You're done! Once you've mastered this method, try some different techniques. Your bean-cooking friends will swear by this or that method. You should listen to their advice, keeping in mind there are few absolutes when cooking beans and it takes very hard work to mess up a pot of beans.

# VARIATIONS

### Slow Cooker

If I'm away from home all day and want beans for dinner, a slow cooker is a super appliance. In the morning I make the mirepoix, add it to the slow cooker along with about ½ pound of beans and some water, and turn the heat to high. The beans are ready by dinner. The problem is that different models have variable heat settings, so your beans may be done in just a few hours or they could take all day. Another drawback is that the top remains on the cooker, allowing very little evaporation. The prized pot liquor (or bean broth) is often thin and lifeless compared with the broth produced when beans are cooked on the stove top.

### Pressure Cooker

Imagine skipping all of these instructions and having beans within an hour of thinking about them! No soaking, no fussing, just delicious beans. Well, almost. You'll need to check the specific instructions for your pressure cooker, but for most models, you can cook unsoaked beans for 20 minutes, slow release, and then open the lid. The beans, though probably done, may have a bland, canned flavor. Deborah Madison, whose cookbooks have inspired many of us, taught me to "finish" the pot by opening the lid and cooking the beans another 20 minutes in the open air, which helps the liquid evaporate a bit and breathes some more life into the beans. Be warned: Using a pressure cooker is quick and easy, but it changes the texture of the beans. If you plan to make refried beans or a purée, this won't matter much, but if you're serving whole beans, I don't recommend a pressure cooker.

### Clay Pot Cooking

Paula Wolfert, author of so many great books on Mediterranean cooking, introduced me to the thrills of cooking with a clay pot. If I have the time, this is my favorite way to cook beans. You need a special pot that can go over direct heat on the stove top. On every trip to Mexico or Italy, I come home with something breakable and beautiful on my lap. Happily, many good cookware stores and ethnic specialty markets have started carrying clay pots. When you find a good bean pot, make sure it's lead-free and follow the manufacturer's instructions for curing it. In the absence of directions, soak the pot overnight in a sink of water, remove it, and drain it. Fill it with 2 cups of water and then cure it in a 250°F oven with a couple of garlic cloves for 2 hours. If you use the pot regularly, there's no need to cure it again. It's a good idea to repeat the curing if you haven't used the pot in about a year.

## The Parsons Method

Just when I thought I knew it all, along comes a new way to cook beans. Russ Parsons of the *Los Angeles Times*, and author of *How to Pick a Peach*, has come up with a technique that takes the best from several different methods. I think this is a great way to cook beans.

"First, I'd like to be specific about what I was trying to do with my bean-cooking experiments: I was not trying to come up with the one and only perfect method for cooking beans (though for most purposes, I think this will suffice). Rather, I was just exploring different ways to get around the problem of pre-soaking. As a lifelong bean-lover and procrastinator, that had always vexed me. What I found was that all of the supposed physiological reasons for soaking beans really did nothing to relieve the digestive problems that usually ensue from eating them. When I went to test that (one day, home alone), I cooked the beans as simply as I could to eliminate any side factors. And I found out that beans cooked that way tasted really, really good. They are meatier and the broth is more profoundly 'beany' than beans that have been soaked."

Essentially, the method comes down to this:

"Put 1 pound of beans in a cast-iron Dutch oven with 6 cups of water and 1 teaspoon of salt. Bring to a simmer on top of the stove and then cover it tightly and pop it into a 350°F oven to bake until the beans are done. This can take anywhere from an hour to 2 hours, depending on the type of bean and how dried out it is. I have used this technique on almost any kind of bean you can think of, from pinquitos to Good Mother Stallard. The one exception I've found is garbanzos, which take so long to cook they really do need to be soaked. You can add seasonings as you wish—I've always got some kind of pork in the pot, and onions and garlic, too. None of those make a difference in the cooking. Other ingredients that are either strongly acidic or alkaline, such as tomatoes and molasses, should be added when the beans are closer to done. In fact, since I came up with the technique, I have added one refinement: at Steve's urging, I started adding the salt halfway through the cooking time and I have found that it reduces splitting but still seasons the beans throughout."

Russ mentions garbanzos as an exception and I might add runner beans like scarlet runners or runner cannellini to the list of beans that need to be soaked no matter what.

As you can see, there are few absolutes with beans. You'll need to experiment on your own and find out which method works for you, your beans, your pots, your water, your humidity, and the way you cook.

# A BIOGRAPHY
## OF A POT OF BEANS

**SO YOU'VE MADE A POT OF BEANS.** There's a sense of accomplishment in that. I always feel as if there was a bit of a struggle between the rock-hard beans and me, and I won! Almost always, the first thing I do is eat a victory bowl for myself. I do this if the beans are all I have for dinner or if I am preparing a complicated menu. As the cook, I'm going to take a minute and enjoy a bowl of beans. I carefully ladle out a cup or so and then I drizzle my favorite extra-virgin olive oil over the top. A spoonful of Parmesan cheese and a mere sprinkle of chopped parsley complete the dish. I take a bite and I feel like I'm eating beans for the first time. The pot liquor is rich and savory, tasting of beans and aromatic vegetables. The beans themselves can be creamy or velvety or soft, depending on the variety. I can't think of anything better. This bowl of beans, a salad, and some crusty bread are the equivalent to food, drink, and lodging in my world.

If I'm in a Latin or Mexican mood, I top the beans with some chopped white onion and a squeeze of key lime. Chopped cilantro, just a bit, works well, too. The main point is that the beans are the stars of the show. A salad works well as a side dish, and warm corn tortillas make the whole affair taste like home.

I could do this every day until the beans are gone, but even I need a little variety. You can incorporate your cooked beans into another, more elaborate dish, like one of the many recipes in this book. Or you can drain them and use them as an ingredient in a mixed salad or soup. If you drain them, save the pot liquor and use it for making soups, cooking vegetables, or even poaching eggs. You can take a cup of the cooked beans and some of their broth and mash them with some onions and lard or oil until you have refried beans that taste nothing like the canned. You can use the puréed beans as a bed for a chicken breast or a rack of lamb. When you get down toward the bottom of the pot and your creativity is challenged, purée the beans with some caramelized onion and make a delicious spread for crostini. Drizzle with some olive oil and finish with a sprinkle of chopped parsley.

# BUYING AND STORING
## BEANS

**OBVIOUSLY, THE BEST WAY** to buy beans is from a grower, but this isn't always practical. Check your local farmers' market and see if there's someone growing heirlooms. Ask the market manager if you don't see any beans. A farmer may just grow one crop of cranberry beans among all his or her other crops. The Internet is also a good place to find beans. My business is odd because I'm trying to encourage people to try New World foods so I have lots of varieties, but it's not uncommon for a grower to specialize in only one or two beans. Specialty-food stores often have heirloom varieties. Be a pest and ask the clerks how old the beans are. Let them know you're done accepting inferior beans!

Grocery stores are more problematic. Black beans are about as exotic as it gets, but the big chains have a lot of competition now. If you let your store manager know what you want, you may be surprised by the results.

Store your beans in an airtight container in a dark cupboard or pantry. It's best to use them within two years. They may be fine several years beyond that.

# TIPS, TECHNIQUES, AND NOTES

## Roasting Chiles and Peppers

In Mexican and Italian cooking, it's common to roast peppers by blistering the skin and peeling it. Off the top of my head, I can't think of an instance when you wouldn't roast a poblano in Mexican cooking. You can roast chiles and peppers right on the grate over a high flame if you have a gas range, turning them occasionally with tongs to cook them evenly. It goes very fast, about 5 minutes per pepper. This method keeps the chiles or peppers nicely firm, while charring the skins perfectly for easy peeling.

If you don't have a gas stove, or if you have a batch of chiles or peppers, roast them in the oven. This method doesn't yield quite the same deep, smoky flavor, and you have to be careful not to let them get mushy. It's fine if you're making a big batch of *chili verde* or any dish in which the chiles will be mixed with a lot of other tasty ingredients in a big pot. Simply preheat the broiler and put the chiles on a baking sheet directly underneath the flame. Roast for 8 to 10 minutes, turning occasionally with tongs so they char evenly.

The final method is to use a *comal* (see page 31) or a dry cast-iron skillet over medium-high heat. You won't have to watch them too closely. Just turn them every once in a while. The disadvantage of this method is that sometimes little divots in the skin don't roast thoroughly, making the chiles or peppers hard to peel. Use a kitchen torch to finish off those stubborn little spots, or just leave them.

No matter how you roast your chiles or peppers, you must steam them so that their skins peel off easily. As you finish roasting them, wrap them in a clean kitchen towel or put them in a paper bag, and let stand for about 10 minutes. When they're cool enough to handle, the skins should rub off easily. Try to avoid rinsing roasted chiles or peppers, which dilutes their flavor. If you've steamed them in a towel, the best way to peel them is to rub the skins off with the towel.

## Toasting Spices

The method for toasting spices is the same no matter which spice you're toasting. Put a dry, heavy skillet, such as cast iron or enameled cast iron, over medium heat and add the spices. Toast for 5 to 7 minutes, shaking the pan often to toast evenly. When the spices are done, you should smell a deep, aromatic, toasty aroma. If they begin to smoke or smell acrid, they are burned and should be discarded. Burned spices taste bitter and can ruin a dish.

Remove the spices from the pan and let them cool before grinding in a spice grinder, a clean coffee grinder dedicated to spices, or a mortar with a pestle.

## Preparing Salt-preserved Anchovies

To prepare a salt-preserved anchovy, soak the fish in several changes of water for about 20 minutes. Rinse well and then scrape off the skin with the dull edge of a paring knife. With your fingers, remove the little fin on the top, along with the bones that come with it. Open the anchovy flat so you see two distinct fillets. With a fingernail, lift up the spine and remove it carefully. Brush away any remaining bones. Rinse the fish well and pat dry with paper towels before using.

## Preparing and Cooking Nopales

Bring a medium saucepan of lightly salted water to a boil. Scrape off the sharp spines on the nopal paddles with a sharp knife. Cut off any bruised or damaged spots. A viscous liquid will ooze from the nopal paddles when you cut into them. Rinse the paddles under cold running water. Cut them crosswise into 1/4-inch-thick slices. Cut the slices into pieces about 1 inch long. Cook the nopal pieces in the boiling water until very tender, about 15 minutes. (One trick for reducing sliminess is to cook the paddles with tomatillo husks, but this isn't necessary.) Drain and rinse well under cold, running water.

## Bean Yield

Some of the recipes in this book call for 1 pound or 1/2 pound of beans. Others require cup measurements. You can expect 1 pound of beans to yield around 6 cups of cooked beans.

# NOTES ON
# INGREDIENTS
## AND EQUIPMENT

### Olive Oil

When I cook with olive oil, I use extra-virgin. Most olive oil sold these days worth using is extra-virgin. I use it a lot. Some people say not to use extra-virgin in cooking, but there are a lot of really good brands in an everyday price range, and the thought of two open bottles is too much!

### Vegetable Oil

Vegetable oil is a bit of a minefield. Of course, you can use whatever oil you like, but I have my preferences. I used to love corn oil for Mexican food, but now almost all of it is genetically modified, so I've stopped using it. Ditto for canola oil. I've settled on using olive oil for most dishes, unless a milder flavor is desired. In certain salads and in many Mexican dishes, I use sunflower or safflower oil.

For high-heat cooking, the oil must be refined, because refined oils have a higher smoke point and don't burn as easily as unrefined oils. Neither olive oil nor sunflower oil is suitable for high-heat cooking. For high-heat cooking, I recommend safflower or grape-seed oil. Both have a neutral flavor and a high smoke point. You may avoid this minefield by using your own rendered lard (see sidebar page 110).

### Salt

Kosher salt is almost always used in the recipes in this book. It is reasonably priced and readily available. The flavor is clean, and its texture makes it perfect for almost any dish. Kosher salt gives grilled meats a desirable crust, it adds a nice crunch to salads, and its flakiness lets it dissolve nicely into cooked bean dishes. Most of the recipes in this book require salting to taste, so you can use whichever salt you prefer. Recipes that specify coarse salt (usually for grinding garlic or other ingredients) require kosher or other similarly textured salt. Anywhere a salt measurement is given, the measured salt was kosher. Keep in mind that if you are using a finer salt, 1 teaspoon fine table salt is going to make a saltier dish than 1 teaspoon kosher salt.

### Tomatoes

When tomatoes are in season, use fresh tomatoes for the recipes in this book. High-quality, canned plum tomatoes are an excellent substitute during the months when good tomatoes are not available in stores. All recipes specify fresh or canned plum tomatoes in the ingredient list. If the tomatoes are an integral part of the dish (especially if the dish is Italian), it's worth it to splurge on canned Italian San Marzano tomatoes.

### Bacon

Many of the recipes in this book call for bacon. It's worth it to spend a little extra on high-quality bacon. Look for thick-cut, lean, smoked or cured bacon. Applewood smoked bacon is a good option that is available in most specialty stores and high-end grocery stores.

### Tortillas

As Mexican food gains in popularity, fresh corn tortillas are becoming available everywhere. Check the ingredient list and make sure that it says "corn, water, and lime." Anything else means that shelf life was more important than flavor. Also check for a lurid yellow color. This means that the lime (or Cal) wasn't rinsed well, leaving the tortillas with an unpleasant chemical flavor but allowing for a longer shelf life. Store tortillas in the refrigerator. Heat them in a hot, dry skillet or *comal*.

### Comal

A *comal* is a large skillet without sides or handles. It's a great way to heat tortillas, toast spices and herbs, and even roast chiles. Most often it is made of steel (not stainless steel). There are also cast-iron versions, which take some time to heat up, and clay versions, which aren't as widely distributed. The steel versions are easy to find, and the quick control of the heat is really handy.

### Cast-iron Pots and Pans

Many of the recipes mention a *comal*. It's great to have, but you can cook everything in this book successfully with a 10-inch cast-iron skillet. Enameled cast-iron pots, like those made by Le Creuset or Staub, are my favorites for making beans, after a clay pot.

*chapter*

# 1

# APPETIZERS
## AND
# SNACKS

# BLACK CALYPSO
## AND CAULIFLOWER SPREAD ON TOASTED BREAD

*Serves 8 to 10*

**1 POUND CAULIFLOWER**, cut into florets

**1 CUP DRAINED, COOKED BLACK CALYPSO BEANS** (page 23)

**1 TABLESPOON CAPERS WITH JUICE**

**1 OIL-PACKED ANCHOVY FILLET** (optional)

**SALT AND FRESHLY GROUND PEPPER**

**½-INCH-THICK SLICES CRUSTY ARTISAN BREAD** (1 per person if loaf is fat or round, 2 if loaf is smaller)

**EXTRA-VIRGIN OLIVE OIL** for brushing and drizzling

**CHOPPED FRESH FLAT-LEAF PARSLEY** for garnishing

*One of the best aspects of working at farmers' markets is the trading that vendors do among themselves after the market ends. I normally come home with quite a bounty—often including ingredients I would never consider buying on my own. One farmer gave me a purple cauliflower, and the result is this spread. The purple cauliflower mixed with the dark beans is less than attractive, but the cauliflower and bean combination is really good.*

Preheat the oven to 400°F.

Place a steamer rack over (but not touching) water in a large saucepan. Add the cauliflower, bring to a boil, and cook until soft, about 6 minutes. Remove the cauliflower from the pan, reserving some of the water, and let the cauliflower cool slightly.

Put the cauliflower, beans, capers, anchovy (if using), and a pinch each of salt and pepper in a blender. Blend until smooth. You may need to stir the mixture with a rubber spatula to get the blades going, but try to avoid adding more liquid. If you need more liquid, use the reserved steaming water. Transfer to a bowl. You will have about 2 cups. Taste and adjust the seasonings.

Brush the bread slices with olive oil. Arrange the slices on a baking sheet and toast in the oven until crisp but still tender inside, about 7 minutes.

Spread the bean mixture on the toasted bread. Sprinkle with parsley and then drizzle with olive oil. Serve on a large platter.

**Substitution Note:** Any of the cranberry or runner beans make a fantastic spread for bread, and all will pair well with the flavors here.

# BRUSCHETTA WITH
# CRANBERRY BEANS AND GARLICKY KALE

*Serves 4 to 6*

3 TABLESPOONS EXTRA-VIRGIN OLIVE OIL plus more for brushing

⅓ CUP CHOPPED WHITE or YELLOW ONION

3 GARLIC CLOVES, finely chopped

⅛ TEASPOON CHOPPED FRESH ROSEMARY

1½ CUPS DRAINED, COOKED CRANBERRY BEANS (page 23)

SALT AND FRESHLY GROUND PEPPER

2 BUNCHES KALE, tough stems removed and coarsely chopped

½-INCH-THICK SLICES CRUSTY ARTISAN BREAD (1 per person if loaf is fat or round, 2 if loaf is smaller)

GRATED PECORINO ROMANO CHEESE for garnishing

*Cranberry beans encompass a whole family whose members have in common somewhat thick skins and a light, creamy interior. They are mostly thought of as Italian (borlotti, tongues of fire, etc.), but their roots are in Colombia where they're still eaten today. This dish makes a light lunch with salad or soup, as well as a hearty appetizer.*

Preheat the oven to 400°F.

In a large, heavy skillet over medium heat, warm 1 tablespoon of the olive oil. Add the onion, one-third of the garlic, and the rosemary. Sauté until soft and fragrant, about 10 minutes.

Put the sautéed vegetables and the beans in a food processor and process until smooth, stopping once or twice to scrape down the sides of the bowl. Season to taste with salt and pepper. Put the bean purée in a small skillet or saucepan and warm over low heat. Keep warm. You will have about 2 cups.

In the same skillet you used to sauté the onions and garlic, warm the remaining 2 tablespoons olive oil over medium heat. Add the remaining garlic and sauté until soft and fragrant, about 10 minutes. Do not allow the garlic to brown. Add the kale and stir until it begins to wilt. Partially cover, reduce the heat to medium-low, and cook, stirring occasionally, until the kale is tender, 8 to 10 minutes. Season to taste with salt and pepper. Keep warm.

Brush the bread with olive oil. Arrange the slices on a baking sheet and toast in the oven until crisp but still tender inside, about 7 minutes. Spread the bean mixture on the toasted bread and top with the kale. Sprinkle with pecorino romano. Serve on a platter.

**Substitution Note:** For a more delicately flavored, less robust bruschetta, substitute white runner beans such as cannellini or marrow.

# CANNELLINI BEAN CONFETTI SPREAD

## WITH ROASTED GARLIC

*Serves 15 to 20*

2 CUPS DRAINED, COOKED CANNELLINI BEANS (page 23)

¼ CUP EXTRA-VIRGIN OLIVE OIL, plus more as needed

5 ROASTED GARLIC CLOVES (recipe follows)

5 OUNCES FRESH GOAT CHEESE

⅓ CUP FRESHLY GRATED PARMESAN CHEESE

¼ CUP SNIPPED FRESH CHIVES

⅓ CUP KALAMATA OLIVES, pitted and finely chopped

SALT AND FRESHLY GROUND PEPPER

ASSORTED CRACKERS AND CROSTINI for serving

*I was a fan of Heidi Swanson's website, 101cookbooks.com, for months before it dawned on me she was a vegetarian and writing exclusively about meatless dishes. Her blog led her to a cookbook and then another, and I doubt there is a limit to what she can do. Heidi's concoction is also great as a ravioli filling.*

In a large mortar with a pestle, or in a large bowl with a potato masher, mash together the beans, ¼ cup olive oil, and roasted garlic until a thick, chunky paste forms. Work in the goat cheese until it is incorporated. Stir in the Parmesan, chives, and olives. Stir in a bit more olive oil, a little at a time, until the spread is thick but still moist. Season generously with salt and pepper. You will have about 3 cups. Serve at room temperature with assorted crackers and crostini for dipping.

**Roasted Garlic:** Preheat the oven to 375°F. Cut off the top third of a garlic head and discard. Drizzle the cut surface with olive oil and sprinkle with salt. Wrap the head tightly in a large piece of aluminum foil. Roast on the middle rack of the oven until the garlic begins to soften and brown, about 45 minutes. Peel back the foil a bit and continue to roast the garlic until it is a deep, nut brown and very soft, 10 to 20 additional minutes. You can roast multiple heads of garlic at the same time for different uses. To remove garlic cloves from the head, wait until the garlic is cool enough to handle and gently squeeze the head, holding it cut side down. The individual cloves should pop out.

**Substitution Note:** Any creamy, meaty bean will work here. Try substituting marrow, *cellini*, or flageolet beans.

# SPICY TEPARY BEAN DIP

*Serves 8 to 10*

---

1½ CUPS DRAINED, COOKED TEPARY BEANS (page 23)

2 GARLIC CLOVES

2 TABLESPOONS EXTRA-VIRGIN OLIVE OIL

1 POBLANO CHILE, roasted (page 29)

¾ TEASPOON CUMIN SEEDS, toasted and ground (page 29)

1 CHIPOTLE CHILE IN ADOBO

SALT AND FRESHLY GROUND PEPPER

*Teparies make an exceptionally rich, out-of-the-ordinary dip that almost tastes Mediterranean, even when made with Latin ingredients. This dip is a versatile addition to any menu: Smear some between two flour tortillas along with grated cheese and salsa and make a quesadilla for serving alongside vegetable soup, or use as a stuffing for roasted mushrooms, topped with crumbled feta cheese and a sprinkling of paprika. You can also serve the dip warm as a snack with tortilla or pita chips and a garnish of chopped fresh cilantro and grated cheese.*

In a food processor, combine the beans, garlic, olive oil, poblano chile, cumin, chipotle chile, and salt and pepper to taste. Process until smooth, stopping once or twice to scrape down the sides of the bowl. You will have about 2 cups. Serve at room temperature.

**Substitution Note:** Nothing tastes quite like tepary beans, but Rio Zape beans have a similar sweetness. Pinto beans will work nicely, too.

## Masa and Masa Harina

Masa means simply "dough," but in Mexican cooking, it's often assumed to mean a *nixtamalized* corn dough. *Nixtamal*, the dough for tortillas and tamales, is prepared by soaking whole kernels of dry, starchy corn in a bath of water and Cal, the mineral lime. The skins are removed, and the corn rinsed and then ground into dough. Using the dough yields the tastiest tortillas and tamales. This classic pre-Columbian technique is labor-intensive and not something a casual cook is likely to take on. Many cities with a large Mexican population have real *tortillerias* that make their masa the old-fashioned way. Sadly, the trend in the United States, and in Mexico as well, is to use an instant masa mix, called masa harina, both commercially and at home.

Masa comes in a fine grind for tortillas and a coarser grind for tamales. If you want to make tortillas, you only need to form the tortillas from the masa. Tamales require fat and, more often than not, chicken broth, along with the coarser grind of masa. Some suppliers offer a masa with these ingredients already incorporated into the dough. Others sell the coarse grind with nothing added. It's important to know what you're getting.

Masa harina, the instant mix, isn't a bad product so don't be dismayed if it's the only one you can find. Follow the instructions on the package and use as you would fresh masa in any recipe.

# REFRIED BEAN MASA EMPANADAS
## WITH ROASTED SALSA VERDE

*Serves 8*

*My idea of heaven is walking around in a foreign city with a few hours to kill and discovering new foods that benefit from being deep-fried. My first taste of Mexican empanadas in Mexico City was eye-opening, and I've been experimenting ever since. I was strolling around the Basilica of Guadalupe in Mexico City and saw a woman making empanadas and frying them on a drum, right on the busy street. The principles of hygiene and the desire for fried masa clashed in my head, but the masa won.*

*Fresh masa almost seems alive the way yeast dough does. It's the very essence of corn, and although it's perfect on its own, something even more wonderful happens when you fry it. The inside cooks but stays soft and voluptuous, while the outside crisps. Whether you're making simple flautas or these rather indulgent masa treats, fried masa is hard to beat. The filling is basically beans but since I'm always keen on gilding the lily, I tried adding cheese and sour cream. Even for me it was too much. As often is the case, the beans don't need our help! They are great on their own. Empanadas are a fine way to use leftover beans.*

**1 POUND FRESH MASA**

**¾ CUP REFRIED BEANS** (page 112)

**SAFFLOWER** or **GRAPESEED OIL** for frying

**MEXICAN *CREMA*** or **SOUR CREAM** for serving (optional)

**ROASTED SALSA VERDE** (page 55) for serving

For each empanada, pinch off a walnut-sized piece of masa and roll into a ball. Place it in a tortilla press between 2 sheets of plastic wrap and press down until you have a 5-inch circle. Place a scant tablespoonful of beans on each circle and fold in half. Roll and press the edges together to seal. As you form the empanadas, put them on a plate and cover them with a damp towel so they don't dry out. You will have about 16 empanadas.

Preheat the oven to 225°F. Line a baking sheet with paper towels.

Pour oil to a depth of ½ inch into a small, heavy skillet set over medium-high heat. Heat the oil until it is shimmering and a small piece of masa placed in the oil sizzles on contact. If the masa smokes and burns, the oil is too hot. Adjust the heat accordingly. Fry the empanadas a few at a time, turning once, until evenly golden brown, 3 to 4 minutes. Adjust the heat and add more oil if necessary. Be sure to allow the oil to come up to temperature before cooking more empanadas. Place the cooked empanadas on the paper towel–lined baking sheet and keep warm in the oven. Serve hot on a platter with *crema* (if using) and salsa.

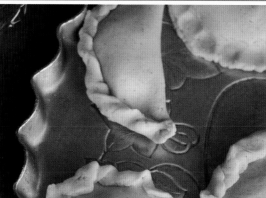

# BEAN-STUFFED PUPUSAS
## WITH CURTIDO

*Serves 4 to 6*

### CURTIDO

½ HEAD GREEN CABBAGE

1 LARGE CARROT, peeled

½ MEDIUM WHITE ONION, very thinly sliced

4 CUPS BOILING WATER

½ CUP WHITE VINEGAR

¼ CUP COLD WATER

2 TEASPOONS SALT

2 TEASPOONS DRIED MEXICAN OREGANO

2 PINCHES OF RED PEPPER FLAKES, or to taste

*As a young fellow in San Francisco, I spent my Sundays in the Mission District. I'd meet my friends at a rather "rustic" watering hole that had an open backyard patio and some of the best live salsa music anywhere. People of all ages came and danced the late afternoon and early evening away, while swigging really bad margaritas and cheap beer. Afterward, the crowd would move to one of the nearby* pupuserias *for a big plate of* pupusas *with pickled cabbage and refried beans, washed down with more beer and gossip about the happenings on the dance floor. For me it was an ideal urban experience. A former Irish neighborhood with Cuban music, Salvadorian food, and Mexican drinks.*

*Pupusas aren't hard to make as long as you don't rush them. Traditionally, the filling is cheese, meat, or loroco (similar to a squash blossom). For this version, the* pupusas *are filled with gorgeous heirloom beans. Be patient with yourself as it takes a few tries to get the hang of patting the masa to the correct thickness around the filling and also to get the temperature on the griddle or* comal *just right so the* pupusas *cook without drying out. Make the pickled cabbage,* curtido, *a few hours ahead. If you don't have access to fresh masa, follow the instructions on a bag of masa harina for tortillas.*

**Make the *curtido*:** Bring the water to a boil. Using a sharp knife, slice the cabbage as thinly as possible. Grate the carrot on the large holes of a box grater. In a large bowl, combine the cabbage, carrot, and onion. Pour the boiling water over the vegetables and push down on them with a wooden spoon to submerge completely. Let sit for 5 minutes. Drain the vegetables, cool, and squeeze lightly to remove the excess water. Return them to the bowl and add the vinegar, cold water, salt, oregano, and red pepper flakes. Toss to combine and chill for 2 to 4 hours. The *curtido* can be made 1 day ahead.

## PUPUSAS

**3 POUNDS FRESH MASA** (page 39)

**1½ TO 2 CUPS REFRIED BEANS** (page 112)

**ABOUT ½ POUND MONTEREY JACK, *QUESO OAXACA*,** or ***QUESO PANELA***, grated

**SAFFLOWER OR GRAPESEED OIL** for frying

**HOT SAUCE** for serving (optional)

**Make the *pupusas*:** For each *pupusa*, pinch off a piece of masa about the size of a medium lemon and roll into a ball. Make an indentation in the ball with your thumb and fill it with a scant 1 tablespoon beans and 2 teaspoons grated cheese. Pinch the dough over the filling and press to seal. Using your palms, flatten the dough into a disk and pat it gently until it is about 5 inches in diameter and about ¼ inch thick. If your hands stick to the masa, moisten them with a little water. As you form the *pupusas*, put them on a plate and cover them with a damp towel so they don't dry out. You will have about 15 *pupusas*.

Preheat the oven to 225°F. Line a heatproof platter with paper towels.

Lightly oil a griddle, large, heavy skillet, or *comal* and heat over medium-high heat. Gently place the *pupusas* in the pan, working in batches to avoid crowding, and cook, turning once, until golden brown and no longer doughy, 6 to 8 minutes. Adjust the heat if needed: if it is too low, the *pupusas* will begin to crack and dry out before they are cooked; if it is too high, they will begin to get little burnt spots before they are cooked. Place the cooked *pupusas* on the paper towel–lined platter and keep warm in the oven. Serve the *pupusas* hot topped with the *curtido* and bottled hot sauce if you like.

# WILD RICE AND WHITE BEAN CANAPÉS

*Serves 8 to 10*

### VINAIGRETTE

1 TABLESPOON FRESH LEMON JUICE

1 TABLESPOON RED WINE VINEGAR

1 TEASPOON DIJON MUSTARD

1 GARLIC CLOVE, finely chopped

2 TABLESPOONS EXTRA-VIRGIN OLIVE OIL

SALT AND FRESHLY GROUND PEPPER

2 TABLESPOONS EXTRA-VIRGIN OLIVE OIL

¼ CUP FINELY CHOPPED WHITE or YELLOW ONION

2 GARLIC CLOVES, finely chopped

3 TABLESPOONS FINELY CHOPPED FRESH FLAT-LEAF PARSLEY

¾ CUP DRAINED, COOKED CREAMY WHITE BEANS such as cannellini or marrow (page 23)

SALT AND FRESHLY GROUND PEPPER

¼ CUP COOKED WILD RICE

2 SMALL PLUM TOMATOES, finely diced

20 CRACKERS OR CROSTINI

*One summer, a bumper crop of tomatoes and some leftover beans and cooked wild rice all came together to make these canapés. The creaminess of the puréed beans highlights the great texture of the cooked wild rice. You need only a small amount of beans and wild rice to make this fantastic appetizer, so it's an ideal way to use leftovers, but it's good enough to warrant cooking a small batch of wild rice.*

**Make the vinaigrette:** In a small bowl, whisk together the lemon juice, vinegar, mustard, garlic, and olive oil. Season to taste with salt and pepper. Set aside.

In a small saucepan over medium heat, warm the olive oil. Sauté the onion and garlic until soft and fragrant, about 10 minutes. Let cool slightly. Transfer to a food processor. Add the parsley and beans. Process until smooth and season to taste with salt and pepper.

In a small bowl, toss the wild rice in half of the vinaigrette and season to taste with salt and pepper. In another small bowl, toss the tomatoes in the remaining vinaigrette, and season with salt and pepper.

Spread the bean mixture on the crackers. Top with a little of the wild rice and then with some of the tomatoes. Arrange on a platter and serve.

# VALLARTA BEANS AND CRABMEAT

## WITH HERBED OIL AND ENDIVE

*Serves 6*

½ CUP PLUS 2 TABLESPOONS EXTRA-VIRGIN OLIVE OIL

2 TEASPOONS CHOPPED FRESH OREGANO

2 TEASPOONS CHOPPED FRESH THYME

1 TABLESPOON SNIPPED FRESH CHIVES

2 TABLESPOONS CHOPPED FRESH FLAT-LEAF PARSLEY

½ CUP CHOPPED YELLOW or WHITE ONION

2 GARLIC CLOVES, minced

1½ CUPS DRAINED, COOKED VALLARTA BEANS (page 23), with reserved broth

1 TEASPOON CHAMPAGNE VINEGAR

SALT AND FRESHLY GROUND PEPPER

6 OUNCES FRESH CRABMEAT or QUALITY CANNED CRABMEAT (see note)

4 HEADS ENDIVE, separated into individual leaves

*I always want to use Vallarta beans when I cook, but the texture is so thick and dense—almost like peanut butter—that I tend to have them only with sautéed greens. One Christmas I puréed a batch and used it for a filling in ravioli topped with a simple sauce of sage butter. This dip is another great inspiration and makes for a dramatic presentation.*

In a small saucepan over medium heat, warm the ½ cup olive oil until it is warm to the touch but not too hot and a pinch of chopped herbs dropped into the oil sizzles just a bit. When the oil is the correct temperature, stir in the oregano, thyme, chives, and parsley. Remove from heat and let steep.

In a medium, heavy skillet over medium heat, warm the 2 tablespoons olive oil. Add the onion and garlic and sauté until soft and fragrant, about 10 minutes. Add the beans along with some of the broth. You want the mixture to be moist, but not soupy. Simmer for about 10 minutes to blend the flavors. Add the vinegar and salt and pepper to taste. Let cool slightly.

In a food processor, purée the bean mixture until smooth, stopping once or twice to scrape down the sides of the bowl. Taste and adjust the seasonings with salt and pepper.

Mound the puréed beans in a serving bowl, top with the crabmeat, and drizzle with the herbed oil. Serve the endive leaves alongside for dipping. Alternatively, put a spoonful of puréed beans in each endive leaf. Top with some crabmeat, drizzle the filled leaves with herbed oil, and serve on a platter. Leftover herbed oil can be stored in the refrigerator for up to 2 weeks and used for salads.

**Note:** The only canned crab that is suitable for this recipe is the high-quality crabmeat sold refrigerated near or among the fresh seafood in grocery and specialty stores. Most canned crab on grocery shelves is inferior in texture, overly salty, and "tinny" tasting.

**Substitution Note:** Any firm bean that has a thin skin and creamy texture will work for this dish. Try cannellini, flageolet, or *mayacoba*.

# SARDINE CONSERVE, WHITE BEANS,
## AND AVOCADOS

*Serves 4*

### SARDINE CONSERVE

SALT

1 POUND FRESH SARDINES (ABOUT 10), cleaned (see note)

⅓ CUP SAFFLOWER or GRAPESEED OIL

½ CUP EXTRA-VIRGIN OLIVE OIL, or as needed

2 GARLIC CLOVES, finely chopped

½ TEASPOON RED PEPPER FLAKES

8 TO 10 CUMIN SEEDS, lightly crushed in a mortar with a pestle

1 TABLESPOON CHOPPED FRESH MARJORAM or OREGANO

2 TABLESPOONS FRESH LEMON JUICE

*When you enter the Opera Bar in Mexico City, your eyes immediately dart around the room looking for the historic bullet holes left by Pancho Villa during the Mexican Revolution. The bar also features a large selection of tequilas and a good kitchen. I was there with some friends late one night when we were served a platter of canned sardines, avocados, and pickled sliced chiles. Maybe I was a little tipsy but it was an epiphany. The creamy, nutty avocado was a great companion to the oily sardines, and the vinegary chiles gave the sardines an edge. As soon as I got home, I repeated the snack, adding white beans to the mix. It's the perfect platter for last-minute guests or a late-night dinner. The sardine conserve needs to be prepared one day ahead, but you can use two four-ounce cans of sardines packed in oil. If opting for canned sardines, add two finely chopped garlic cloves to the beans.*

**To make the sardine conserve:** Lightly salt the sardines. In a heavy 10- or 12-inch skillet over medium-high heat, warm the ⅓ cup safflower oil. Working in batches, fry the sardines, turning once, until cooked through, about 10 seconds per side. Drain on paper towels. In a small bowl, whisk together the ½ cup olive oil, garlic, red pepper flakes, cumin, marjoram, and lemon juice. Pour half of the olive oil mixture into a shallow glass or ceramic dish measuring about 4 by 5 inches. Put the sardines in the dish, packing them tightly and layering them if necessary. Pour the remaining olive oil mixture over the sardines, shaking the dish to make sure all the sardines are submerged. Add a little more olive oil if needed to cover the fish. Cover the dish and refrigerate for 24 hours. The sardines will keep in the refrigerator up to 5 days.

1½ CUPS DRAINED, COOKED WHITE BEANS SUCH AS MARROW, CANNELLINI, or *CELLINI* (page 23), warmed

¼ CUP CHOPPED SWEET ONION

3 TABLESPOONS CHOPPED FRESH CILANTRO

1 TABLESPOON CIDER VINEGAR or MILD WHITE WINE VINEGAR

3 TABLESPOONS EXTRA-VIRGIN OLIVE OIL

SALT AND FRESHLY GROUND PEPPER

BUTTER LETTUCE LEAVES

2 AVOCADOS, pitted, peeled, and sliced

"TACO TRUCK" PICKLED JALAPEÑOS AND CARROTS (page 140)

CORN TORTILLAS, heated

In a medium bowl, toss the beans with the onion and cilantro. Put the cider vinegar in a small bowl. Slowly whisk in the olive oil in a thin stream. Season to taste with salt and pepper. Pour over the beans and toss.

Make a bed of lettuce leaves on a platter. Drain the marinated sardines. Arrange the beans, sardines, and sliced avocados in little piles on top of the leaves. Garnish with the pickled jalapeños and carrots. Serve the tortillas on the side.

**Note:** To clean fresh sardines, use the dull edge of a paring knife to scrape off any loose scales from each fish. Firmly grasp the head and pull. Most of the viscera will come out with the head. With a sharp paring knife, cut down the length of the belly, rinsing away any remaining viscera. Grasp the top fin between your index finger and thumb and pull sharply toward the head. It should come off easily. Pull out the little bone that runs across the top of the fish. Carefully open the fish flat from the belly side, exposing the entire backbone. Run an index finger under the backbone to separate it from the flesh, working your way slowly toward the tail. Pull sharply, removing the tail as well. Rinse the sardines and pat them dry.

# CELLINIS AND MARTINIS

*Serves 4*

1½ CUPS DRAINED, COOKED *CELLINI* BEANS (page 23), warmed

2 GARLIC CLOVES, finely chopped

3 TABLESPOONS FINELY CHOPPED FRESH FLAT-LEAF PARSLEY

½ TEASPOON FINELY CHOPPED FRESH ROSEMARY

3 TABLESPOONS EXTRA-VIRGIN OLIVE OIL

1 TABLESPOON RED WINE VINEGAR

RED PEPPER FLAKES

SALT AND FRESHLY GROUND PEPPER

## MARTINIS

ICE CUBES

1½ TABLESPOONS NOILLY PRAT or OTHER FINE VERMOUTH

1 CUP OF THE BEST GIN YOU CAN AFFORD

4 OLIVES or LEMON TWISTS

*Long before I got into agriculture and food, my passions were cocktails and jazz, two less nourishing but no less important New World treats. To me, a martini meant gin and vermouth stirred over ice and then strained into a chilled cocktail glass. Now the drink seems to be whatever finds its way into in a classic cocktail glass. Here is my preferred martini, which will be enhanced by listening to Vince Guaraldi or some other classic West Coast jazz and serving this tapas plate. Since jazz is the music of choice, you can improvise by adding what's on hand, such as anchovies, cubed sheep cheese, or prosciutto.*

In a medium bowl, combine the beans, garlic, parsley, rosemary, olive oil, vinegar, and red pepper flakes to taste. Toss to combine. Season to taste with salt and pepper. Marinate at room temperature for 1 hour before serving. The beans can be marinated in the refrigerator for up to 2 days. Bring to room temperature before serving, and taste and adjust the seasonings.

**Make the martinis:** Place 4 long-stemmed cocktail glasses and a glass pitcher in the freezer to chill for at least 1 hour, preferably all day.

Remove the pitcher from the freezer and fill with ice cubes. Pour the vermouth over the cubes and stir with a glass stirring rod, covering each cube with vermouth. Strain the vermouth, leaving only the cubes in the pitcher.

Pour the gin over the cubes in the pitcher. Stir gently but firmly until the gin is well chilled. Strain into the chilled glasses. Garnish each drink with an olive or a lemon twist.

**Note:** There is no such thing as a vodka martini. There may be a vodka-vermouth drink that you enjoy, but it is not a martini.

**Substitution Note:** *Cellini* beans work well in this recipe because they are huge and soft and don't fall apart easily. You could substitute scarlet runner beans or any other runner beans but they won't be quite as soft or as nice looking.

# ZUZU'S
# YELLOW INDIAN WOMAN
## FRITTERS

*Serves 10 to 12*

**2 CUPS DRAINED, COOKED YELLOW INDIAN WOMAN BEANS** (page 23)

**¼ CUP WHOLE MILK**

**¼ SMALL RED ONION**

**1 CUP YELLOW CORNMEAL**, or more if needed

**⅓ CUP ALL-PURPOSE FLOUR**

**1 TABLESPOON SUGAR**

**½ CUP BUTTERMILK**, or more if needed

**1 EGG**, beaten

**2 TABLESPOONS CHOPPED FRESH CILANTRO**

**GRATED ZEST OF 1 LIME**

**1½ TEASPOONS COARSE SALT**

**½ TEASPOON FRESHLY GROUND PEPPER**

**SAFFLOWER** or **GRAPESEED OIL** for frying

**CLASSIC RED SALSA** (page 57) for serving

**SOUR CREAM** for serving

*Chef Angela Tamura has made Zuzu one of the most popular destinations in Napa. It's one of those rare spots where both locals and tourists feel comfortable. Much of that has to do with Angela's hands in the kitchen. These fritters make a great starter. I don't know what Angela would think, but I've even served them on top of a mixed green salad.*

In a food processor, purée 1½ cups of the beans, the milk, and the onion until a smooth paste forms, stopping once or twice to scrape down the sides of the bowl.

In a large bowl, using a potato masher, mash the remaining ½ cup beans until they are smooth with some texture remaining. Add the beans from the food processor, 1 cup cornmeal, flour, sugar, ½ cup buttermilk, egg, cilantro, lime zest, salt, and pepper. Mix well with a rubber spatula. The texture should be like that of oatmeal. Add more cornmeal or buttermilk if needed.

Preheat the oven to 225°F. Line a baking sheet with paper towels.

Pour the safflower oil to a depth of about ½ inch into a medium, heavy skillet. Put over high heat and heat the oil until it is very hot and shimmering, but not smoking. A scant teaspoon of bean batter placed in the oil should hold its shape and sizzle on contact. If it smokes and burns, the oil is too hot. Adjust the heat accordingly.

Working in batches of about 6 fritters, drop the bean batter by scant tablespoons into the oil, being careful not to crowd the pan, and cook until the fritters are set and browned on the bottom, about 1 minute. Carefully turn them with tongs or a metal spatula and cook on the second side for 1 minute. The fritters should be set and turn a dark caramel brown. Place the fritters on the paper towel–lined baking sheet and keep warm in the oven. Adjust heat and add more oil if needed. Let the oil come to temperature before cooking more fritters. You will have about 25 fritters.

Arrange the fritters on a platter and accompany with salsa and sour cream.

**Substitution Note:** Any of the firm beans that purée nicely are perfect here. Try Vallartas or pintos.

# RUBICON'S
# MARROW BEANS AND MARROW BONES
## WITH CARAMELIZED GARLIC AND CIPOLLINI ONIONS

*Serves 8*

**¾ POUND MARROW BEANS**, soaked (page 21)

**1 MEDIUM CARROT**, peeled and finely chopped

**2 CELERY STALKS**, finely chopped

**1 MEDIUM YELLOW ONION**, finely chopped

**SALT**

**12 GARLIC CLOVES**, halved lengthwise

*Rubicon is a great restaurant that has undergone somewhat of a renaissance. This is in no small part to the efforts of chef Stuart Brioza and his team. I've watched Stuart absorb information about a bean and then come back a week later and describe an out-of-this-world creation that makes the most out of the particular bean's assets. This dish is no exception. You can leave the marrow bones out and serve it as a side dish for braised meats or as a stand-alone entrée. If using the marrow bones, ask your butcher to cut them for you.*

Put the beans and their soaking water and the carrot, celery, and onion in a large soup pot. Add enough cold water to cover by at least 1 inch. Bring to a boil, reduce the heat to low, and simmer, uncovered, until the beans are soft, about 1½ hours. Remove from the heat, add salt to taste, and let the beans cool in their broth. The beans can be cooked up to 2 days ahead. Store in the refrigerator in their broth.

About 45 minutes before you plan to serve the dish, preheat the oven to 400°F.

Bring a small saucepan of water to a boil. Add the garlic and cook for 2 minutes. Drain, and repeat two more times, changing the water each time. This process mellows the harsh heat of the garlic. Set aside.

Drain beans, reserving the broth. Put the beans in a large saucepan and warm over low heat, adding a little of the reserved broth to keep them from sticking to the pan.

½ CUP EXTRA-VIRGIN OLIVE OIL

12 *CIPOLLINI* ONIONS or SHALLOTS, halved

FRESHLY GROUND PEPPER

2 CUPS DRY RED WINE

3 TABLESPOONS UNSALTED BUTTER

EIGHT 2-INCH PIECES OF MARROW BONE

¼ CUP FRESH FLAT-LEAF PARSLEY LEAVES

2 TABLESPOONS FRESH MARJORAM LEAVES

8 LARGE SLICES CRUSTY ARTISAN BREAD, toasted

In a large, heavy skillet over high heat, warm ¼ cup of the olive oil. Add the *cipollini* and garlic and sauté until lightly browned, about 5 minutes. Reduce the heat to low and cook, stirring often, until the garlic and *cipollini* are caramelized, golden, and tender, about 30 minutes. Season to taste with salt and pepper. Add the red wine and cook over low heat until the wine thickens and glazes the pan. Add 1 cup of the reserved bean broth and cook until the glaze thickens, about 15 minutes. Add the butter to the warm beans, and then add the beans to the skillet.

Meanwhile, put the marrow bones in an ovenproof dish and coat them generously with the remaining ¼ cup olive oil. Season with salt, toss well, and arrange with the bone, not the marrow, touching the bottom of the dish. Roast until the bones are well browned and the marrow becomes meltingly tender throughout, about 30 minutes.

Place 1 roasted bone in the center of each plate. Spoon some of the bean mixture around it. Garnish with the parsley and marjoram, and season with salt and pepper. Accompany each serving with a slice of toasted bread.

**Substitution Note:** Any of the white beans will work here. Try cannellini or *cellini*.

## Thoughts on Salsa

I am often asked why I don't make a commercial salsa. The main reason is I don't understand why home cooks wouldn't just make their own. It's simple and easy. The recipes that follow are general guidelines. Please improvise based on your taste and what you have on hand. The chiles can be jalapeños or güeros and the lime can be replaced by a fruity vinegar if you like.

# ROASTED *Salsa*
# VERDE

*Makes 2 cups*

1 TEASPOON DRIED MEXICAN OREGANO

5 LARGE TOMATILLOS, husks intact

1 SMALL WHITE or RED ONION, cut into ¼-inch-thick slices

4 LARGE GARLIC CLOVES, unpeeled

2 SERRANO CHILES

JUICE OF 2 KEY LIMES or 1 PERSIAN LIME

SALT

*The roasted flavors in this salsa make it a great companion for anything with beans. It's a snap to throw together in the food processor, but if you want to make salsa the authentic way, grind the roasted ingredients in a traditional molcajete. The wonderful aromas rise up to meet you as you grind by hand, making the preparation an experience to remember. This is the salsa for serving with empanadas (page 40).*

In a dry, heavy skillet or *comal* over medium heat, toast the oregano until fragrant, 1 to 2 minutes. Remove from the skillet and set aside.

In the same skillet over medium-low heat, cook the tomatillos, onion, garlic, and chiles, turning occasionally, until the vegetables are soft and fragrant. You'll need to keep an eye on them so they don't burn. The garlic takes the longest, so put it on the hottest part of the pan. When the vegetables are cool enough to handle, peel the garlic, cut the stems from the chiles, leaving the seeds, and remove the husks from the tomatillos.

In the food processor or blender, combine the oregano, tomatillos, onion, garlic, and chiles. Pulse until well blended, but allow the salsa to retain some texture. Some of the tomatillo pieces should be the size of almonds. Add the lime juice and salt to taste. The salsa will keep for 1 week in the refrigerator.

# THREE-CHILE

*Makes about 2 cups*

## Salsa

**4 FRESH** or **CANNED TOMATILLOS**

**ICE WATER**

**3 GARLIC CLOVES**, 2 unpeeled, 1 peeled

**1 SERRANO CHILE**

**1 POBLANO CHILE**, roasted, peeled, and seeded (page 29)

**1 ANCHO CHILE**, split, seeded, and soaked in warm water to cover for 15 minutes

**5 FRESH** or **CANNED PLUM TOMATOES**, drained

**¾ TEASPOON CUMIN SEEDS**, toasted and ground (page 29)

**ABOUT ½ CUP FRESH CILANTRO LEAVES**

**JUICE OF 2 KEY LIMES** or **1 PERSIAN LIME**

**SALT AND FRESHLY GROUND PEPPER**

*This is what happens when you can't decide whether to make a fresh salsa or a roasted salsa, a red salsa or a green salsa. Depending on the chiles, the salsa might be too hot. To tame the heat, use more tomatoes or tomatillos than the recipe calls for, which will increase your yield.*

If using fresh tomatillos, remove the papery husks. Bring a small saucepan of water to a boil. Add the tomatillos, reduce the heat to low, and simmer for 8 to 10 minutes. Drain and immediately plunge the tomatillos into an ice water bath to stop the cooking. Drain and set aside.

In a dry, heavy skillet or *comal* over medium-high heat, cook the 2 cloves of unpeeled garlic and the serrano chile, turning occasionally, until the garlic is soft and the chile is charred all over. You'll need to keep an eye on them so they don't burn. When they are cool enough to handle, partially seed the chile, leaving about half the seeds, and peel the garlic.

In a blender or food processor, combine the raw and cooked garlic and the serrano and poblano chiles. Drain the ancho chile, reserving 2 tablespoons of the soaking liquid. Add to the blender or food processor along with the tomatoes, tomatillos, cumin, cilantro, and lime juice. Blend or process until smooth. Season to taste with salt and pepper. The salsa will keep for 1 week in the refrigerator.

# CLASSIC RED Salsa

*Makes 1 ¼ cups*

TWO ¼-INCH-THICK SLICES RED ONION

2 GARLIC CLOVES, unpeeled

2 SERRANO CHILES

1 CUP CANNED WHOLE PLUM TOMATOES, drained

¼ CUP CHOPPED FRESH CILANTRO

JUICE OF 2 KEY LIMES or 1 PERSIAN LIME

SALT

*The window when fresh tomatoes are good is narrow, even in California. Rather than make a salsa with unsatisfying hothouse tomatoes, I use canned. The texture of peeled, whole plum tomatoes is best. When great heirloom tomatoes are in season, you can use the real thing.*

In a dry, heavy skillet or *comal* over medium-high heat, cook the onion slices, garlic cloves, and chiles, turning occasionally, until they char. You'll need to keep an eye on them so they don't burn. Remove the vegetables as they finish cooking. The garlic will take the longest. When the garlic cloves are cool enough to handle, peel them.

Put the onion, garlic, chiles, tomatoes, cilantro, and lime juice in a small food processor or blender and pulse until a roughly chopped salsa forms. Season to taste with salt. The salsa will keep for 1 week in the refrigerator.

*chapter*

# 2

# SOUPS, STEWS, AND CHILIES

# BORLOTTI MINESTRONE
## WITH ARUGULA PESTO

*Serves 4 to 6*

3 TABLESPOONS EXTRA-VIRGIN OLIVE OIL

1 SMALL YELLOW ONION, sliced

3 GARLIC CLOVES, finely chopped

1 MEDIUM FENNEL BULB, trimmed and thinly sliced

SALT

½ MEDIUM HEAD GREEN CABBAGE, thinly sliced

5 CUPS CHICKEN BROTH

½ POUND GREEN BEANS, trimmed and cut in half

2 CUPS COOKED *BORLOTTI* BEANS in their broth (page 23)

FRESHLY GROUND PEPPER

### PESTO

3 GARLIC CLOVES

SALT

¼ POUND BABY ARUGULA LEAVES

ABOUT ½ CUP FRESH FLAT-LEAF PARSLEY LEAVES

⅓ CUP EXTRA-VIRGIN OLIVE OIL

½ CUP FRESHLY GRATED PARMESAN CHEESE

2 TO 3 TEASPOONS FRESH LEMON JUICE

FRESHLY GROUND PEPPER

*In the late 1980s, I was living in Italy and hosting a jazz radio show. I like to do things the hard way, apparently, so I did the show live and often included a segment where listeners could call in and request songs or just chat. This would be fine, except my mastery of Italian was less than impressive and I'm sure I sounded somewhat like Charo trying to speak English. The show was based in Milan, but every chance I could, I'd hop on a train to Florence to visit my friends and eat beans. The beans would often be in the form of a rustic vegetable soup like this one. You can vary the vegetables depending on what's in season. In summer, include zucchini and tomatoes; in winter, potatoes and carrots are appropriate.*

In a soup pot over medium heat, warm the olive oil. Add the onion, garlic, fennel, and a pinch of salt and sauté until the vegetables are soft and fragrant, about 10 minutes. Add the cabbage, stir to coat with the oil, and cook until wilted, about 5 minutes. Add the broth and another pinch of salt. Bring to a boil and simmer, uncovered, for 15 minutes. Add the green beans and the *borlotti* beans and simmer for 15 minutes. Season to taste with salt and pepper.

**Meanwhile, make the pesto:** Put the garlic and a pinch of salt in a mortar and pound into a paste with a pestle. Transfer to a food processor. (You may also use the food processor for the first step, but pounding the raw garlic makes it mellow and sweet and creates a texture that integrates well into the pesto.) Add the arugula, parsley, and a pinch of salt. Process until well chopped. With the motor running, slowly drizzle in the olive oil, stopping once to scrape down the sides of the bowl. Add the Parmesan and lemon juice and season to taste with salt and pepper.

Ladle the soup into warmed bowls and top with a dollop of pesto. Store any leftover pesto in the refrigerator for up to 1 week.

**Substitution Note:** Any of the cranberry beans work wonderfully here. For a lighter soup, substitute a white runner bean like a *cellini* or cannellini. If heirlooms are unavailable, use white navy beans.

# TUSCAN RIBOLLITA WITH
# RUNNER CANNELLINI BEANS

*Serves 5 to 6*

1/2 CUP EXTRA-VIRGIN OLIVE OIL

1 MEDIUM YELLOW ONION, chopped

1 CELERY STALK, chopped

3 GARLIC CLOVES, finely chopped

1 MEDIUM CARROT, peeled and chopped

4 CUPS SHREDDED SAVOY CABBAGE

1 BUNCH DINOSAUR KALE, tough stems removed and leaves coarsely chopped

6 CUPS CHICKEN BROTH

SALT AND FRESHLY GROUND PEPPER

2 CUPS DRAINED, COOKED RUNNER CANNELLINI BEANS (page 23)

6 SLICES DAY-OLD HEARTY BREAD, each about 1/2 inch thick, cut from a large loaf

1/2 CUP FRESHLY GRATED PARMESAN CHEESE

*It's amazing how many great bean recipes come from Italy. It's also a marvel how Italian farmers bred New World vegetables like tomatoes and certain bean varieties to their liking, setting a new standard. Although there are many different versions of this peasant soup, the black kale, cavolo nero, is a classic ingredient. Often the kale is labeled as dinosaur kale, and I've even seen it called lacinato.*

In a soup pot over medium heat, warm 1/4 cup of the olive oil. Add the onion, celery, garlic, and carrot and sauté until soft and fragrant, but not brown, about 10 minutes. Add the cabbage and kale and cook, stirring, until well coated and beginning to wilt. Add the broth and season with salt and pepper. Bring to a simmer, cover, and cook until the cabbage and kale are soft, about 1 1/2 hours. The soup is even better made up to this point 1 to 3 days ahead and refrigerated.

Preheat the oven to 400°F.

Bring the soup to a slow simmer and add the beans. Cook for 15 minutes to blend the flavors. Taste and adjust the seasonings. Line the bottom of a 3- or 4-quart Dutch oven or ovenproof baking dish with 2 of the bread slices. Top with half the soup. Lay 2 more bread slices on top of the soup. Add the remaining soup and then the remaining bread slices, pushing down on them to submerge them in the liquid. Drizzle the top evenly with the remaining 1/4 cup olive oil. Top with the Parmesan cheese. Bake until the top is brown and bubbly, 20 to 25 minutes. Spoon into warmed bowls and serve.

**Substitution Note:** Any of the white beans are just fine here. For a heartier soup, use cranberry beans.

# CELLINI BEAN SOUP

## WITH CHARD AND POACHED EGGS

*Serves 4*

½ **POUND *CELLINI* BEANS,** soaked (page 21)

**4 GARLIC CLOVES**

**1 BUNCH GREEN CHARD**

**SALT**

**6 SLICES DAY-OLD HEARTY BREAD** cut from a large loaf, crusts removed

**⅓ CUP PLUS 4 TABLESPOONS EXTRA-VIRGIN OLIVE OIL**

**FRESHLY GROUND PEPPER**

**4 EGGS**

**2 TABLESPOONS WHITE VINEGAR**

*At farmers' markets, you get a real sense of what I'd call "ingredient-driven" chefs. These men and women are at the markets every week, closely watching the changing seasons and planning their menus by what looks best. Some popular chefs give lip service to the concept of seasonal, local food. Others are dedicated to the concept because they know their dishes are only as good as their ingredients. If you come to the Ferry Plaza market in San Francisco early on any given Saturday morning, you're more than likely to see Phil West of the Michelin-starred Range pushing around a big cart of vegetables and a big sack of beans. He's the rare mix of talent, personality, and grace that you just don't find every day, and I'm always flattered that he insists on using my beans and posole for Range.*

Put the beans and their soaking water in a stockpot and add cold water if needed to cover the beans by 1 inch. Put the garlic on a piece of cheesecloth, gather the corners, and tie the bundle securely. Add to the pot.

Put the pot over medium-high heat and bring to a simmer. Reduce the heat to low and slowly cook the beans, uncovered, until tender, 1 to 1½ hours. Add water to the pot as necessary to keep the beans submerged. Gently stir the beans once or twice to prevent them from sticking to the bottom of the pot.

*continued-*

RANGE RESTAURANT'S

# CELLINI BEAN SOUP
## WITH CHARD AND POACHED EGGS

*-continued*

Meanwhile, bring a large saucepan of water to a boil. Remove the chard leaves from inner stems, reserving the stems, and tear the leaves into 1- to 2-inch pieces. Trim the tough outer edges and base of the stems. Slice the stems on the diagonal into thin matchsticks. Generously salt the boiling water. Add the chard leaves and cook until tender, 2 to 3 minutes. Remove with a slotted spoon and transfer to a colander to drain. Repeat with the chard stems. When the chard is cool enough to handle, squeeze gently to remove excess water. Set aside.

Preheat the oven to 350°F. Tear the bread into small pieces and put in a medium bowl. While tossing, drizzle the bread with 2 tablespoons of the olive oil and season with salt and pepper. Put the bread on a baking sheet in a single layer and toast until very crisp and golden brown, 25 to 30 minutes. Let the bread cool on the pan. Crumble the toasted bread if you want smaller pieces.

When the beans are tender, season them with salt and pepper. Remove the cheesecloth bundle from the pot, unwrap, and remove the garlic cloves. Ladle out about half the beans with their broth and put in a blender. Add the garlic cloves and the ⅓ cup olive oil. Purée until smooth. If necessary, blend the hot soup in small batches as it can splatter and burn you. Adjust the liquid remaining in the pot if necessary. For a thinner soup, leave most or all the liquid in the pot; for a thicker soup, remove some liquid. Add the puréed beans to the pot and set over medium heat. Add the chard and chard stems. Taste and adjust the seasonings. Keep warm.

Fill a medium saucepan with cold water and salt the water. Heat the water over medium heat. Break each egg into a cup. When the water is barely simmering, add the vinegar. Slide the eggs, one at a time, into the water, trying to keep the eggs as compact as possible. Cook the eggs until the whites are set and the yolks are still soft, 2 to 3 minutes. Using a slotted spoon, remove each poached egg from the water and place in the middle of a warmed soup bowl. Carefully ladle the soup around the eggs so the yolks stay intact. Sprinkle the soup with the bread, drizzle with the remaining 2 tablespoons olive oil, and season with pepper.

**Substitution Note:** Any of the white runners are perfect here. Try cannellini for a variation.

# MANRESA'S
# COOL WHITE BEAN BOUILLON
## WITH WINE VINEGAR

*Serves 6*

### VEGETABLE BOUILLON

**1 MEDIUM YELLOW ONION**, cut into quarters

**1 LEEK**, white part only, split lengthwise and rinsed

**1 MEDIUM CARROT**, peeled and cut lengthwise into quarters

**3 OR 4 FRESH FLAT-LEAF PARSLEY SPRIGS**

**2 GARLIC CLOVES**

**1 MEDIUM TURNIP**, peeled and cut into quarters

**1 MEDIUM FENNEL BULB**, trimmed and cut into quarters

**2½ QUARTS WATER**

**1 TEASPOON PEPPERCORNS**

**1 TABLESPOON CORIANDER SEEDS**

**3 STAR ANISE**

**1 TABLESPOON SUGAR**

**½ CUP DRY WHITE WINE**

*David Kinch, the Michelin-starred chef and owner of the renowned restaurant Manresa in Los Gatos, is generally considered to be one of the most important chefs in the country, and yet he personally shops the farmers' markets weekly. He isn't above watching my booth while I rush off for a quick break, and he takes all kinds of ribbing while dispensing surfing tips and orating on the virtues of knowing the pH balance of a pot of beans. This dish, which David made especially for this book, is not for a casual weeknight supper. It is crafted to showcase the ingredients and demonstrates David's attention to detail and infectious creativity.*

**Make the bouillon:** Combine the onion, leek, carrot, parsley, garlic, turnip, fennel, water, peppercorns, coriander, star anise, and sugar in a soup pot. Bring to a boil over medium heat, reduce the heat to low, and simmer, uncovered, until vegetables are tender, 45 minutes. Add the wine and let cool completely without straining. The bouillon can be prepared 1 day ahead and refrigerated.

Put the beans in a large pot. Strain the vegetable bouillon and discard the vegetables. Reserve 3 to 4 cups of the bouillon. Add the remaining bouillon to the pot with the beans. Add enough cold water to cover by 1 inch. Bring to a simmer over medium heat, skimming off any foam that rises to the surface. Gently simmer the beans until they are completely soft but retain their shape and firmness, about 1½ hours. Season with salt when the beans are nearly done. Add water if necessary to keep the beans submerged. Let the beans cool in their broth. Drain the beans, reserving the broth. Put about 1 cup of the beans in a small bowl and mash with a fork or potato masher until fairly smooth. Season with salt, 2 tablespoons of the olive oil, and lemon juice to taste. Set aside. Refrigerate the remaining beans.

*continued-*

MANRESA'S
# COOL WHITE BEAN BOUILLON
## WITH WINE VINEGAR

*-continued*

½ **POUND CANNELLINI BEANS**, soaked (page 21) and drained

**SEA SALT**

**8 TABLESPOONS EXTRA-VIRGIN OLIVE OIL**

**JUICE OF 1 LEMON**

**12 SMALL PEARL ONIONS**, peeled

**12 BABY CARROTS**, trimmed

**1 SMALL BUNCH TENDER YOUNG CHARD LEAVES**, sliced into ribbons

**6 BABY SUMMER SQUASH** or **ZUCCHINI**

**FRESHLY GROUND PEPPER**

**ABOUT 3 TABLESPOONS BEST-QUALITY RED WINE VINEGAR**

**3 OUNCES FRESH GOAT CHEESE**

½ **BAGUETTE**, cut on the diagonal into twelve ½-inch slices and toasted

**1 GARLIC CLOVE**, cut in half

**1 TOMATO**, cut in half

**GRATED ZEST OF 1 ORANGE** for garnishing

In a large skillet, bring the reserved vegetable bouillon and reserved bean broth to a simmer over medium-high heat. One at a time, cook the pearl onions, baby carrots, chard, and squash until tender, removing them with a slotted spoon as you go. Add water as needed to cover the vegetables. Chill the vegetables and the bouillon separately. You should have 3 cups bouillon or broth. Add water if you do not.

Season the chilled bouillon to taste with salt and pepper, and add the vinegar. Divide the goat cheese into 18 equal pieces. Use the palms of your hands to form the cheese into little balls. Brush the toasted bread with some of the remaining olive oil and gently rub with the cut sides of the garlic. Rub the tomato halves into the bread slices and top each slice with a small spoonful of the bean purée.

Spoon about ⅓ cup of the beans into each of 6 chilled shallow bowls. Divide the chilled vegetables and goat cheese among the bowls. Pour the seasoned bouillon over the vegetables to cover. Drizzle each serving with 1 tablespoon of the remaining olive oil and garnish with the orange zest. Season with pepper. Accompany with the toasts.

**Substitution Note:** Any white bean will work here, including *cellini* or marrow.

# JIMTOWN STORE'S
# PASTA FAZOOL

*Serves 4*

---

**4 SLICES HIGH-QUALITY BACON**, diced (optional)

**1 TO 3 TABLESPOONS EXTRA-VIRGIN OLIVE OIL**, plus more for serving

**1 MEDIUM YELLOW ONION**, chopped

**1 CELERY STALK**, chopped

**2 GARLIC CLOVES**, finely chopped

**1 SMALL CARROT**, peeled and chopped

**4 CUPS CHICKEN BROTH**

**1 TABLESPOON CHOPPED FRESH OREGANO**

**½ POUND CANNELLINI, MARROW, or *CELLINI* BEANS**, soaked (page 21) and drained

**ONE 14-OUNCE CAN CRUSHED TOMATOES**

**SALT AND FRESHLY GROUND PEPPER**

**1 CUP TINY PASTA SHELLS** or **TUBES**

**¼ CUP CHOPPED FRESH FLAT-LEAF PARSLEY**

**FRESHLY GRATED PARMESAN CHEESE** for serving

*You don't see* pasta e fagioli *on a lot of menus, but it's the best kind of home cooking and a great way to enjoy beans Italian style. This recipe comes from the kitchen of the Jimtown Store in Sonoma's Alexander Valley, where proprietress Carrie Brown holds court. I've known Carrie since the late 1970s (when we were both mere children!), and she's the first person many of us go to with questions about style, taste, trends, and substance. She can look at a table setting, a building, or a bowl of pasta and tell you what works and what doesn't. The combination of beans and noodles might sound odd, but wait until you try it.*

In a soup pot over medium heat, sauté the bacon (if using) until the fat is rendered and the bacon is beginning to brown, 8 to 10 minutes. Remove with a slotted spoon and drain on paper towels.

Pour off all but 2 tablespoons of the fat in the pot. Add 1 tablespoon of the olive oil or 3 tablespoons of the olive oil if not using bacon. Heat over medium heat and add the onion, celery, garlic, and carrot. Sauté until vegetables are soft and fragrant, about 10 minutes. Add the broth, oregano, and beans. Bring to a boil, reduce the heat to low, and simmer, partially covered, until the beans are tender, about 1½ hours. Add the tomatoes. Season the beans with salt and pepper. Add the pasta, raise the heat to medium-high, and cook until the pasta is al dente, adding water if necessary.

Return the bacon (if using) to the pot and stir in the parsley. Taste and adjust the seasonings. Let sit for 10 minutes to allow the flavors to blend. Ladle into warmed bowls, sprinkle with Parmesan, and drizzle with olive oil.

# SENATE BEAN
## SOUP

*Serves 4*

½ **POUND YELLOW EYE BEANS**, soaked (page 21) and drained

**ONE 1½-POUND HAM HOCK**, cut crosswise into 3 or 4 pieces

**6 CUPS WATER**

**1 BAY LEAF**

½ **MEDIUM YELLOW ONION**, chopped

**4 CELERY STALKS WITH LEAVES**, chopped

**2 GARLIC CLOVES**, finely chopped

¼ **CUP CHOPPED FRESH FLAT-LEAF PARSLEY**, plus more for garnishing

**SALT AND FRESHLY GROUND PEPPER**

*When I tell my customers to cook beans simply, they often nod in agreement and say something like, "I'll just cook them with a ham hock." My heart sinks a little. Beans are great with ham hocks, but freshly dried heirloom varieties don't need them. Save the pork for another cause, at least the first time you make heirloom beans. But I do understand the love of ham, and there are times when that old-fashioned comfort combination of beans and ham is required. This simple soup has been served to legislators at the U.S. Senate Restaurant in Washington, DC, since the early 1900s. The authentic version uses navy beans, but an heirloom just makes it better. You can ask your butcher to cut the ham hock for you.*

In a soup pot, combine the beans, ham hock, water, and bay leaf. Bring to a boil, reduce the heat to low, and simmer gently until the beans are beginning to soften, about 1 hour. Add the onion, celery, garlic, ¼ cup parsley, and salt and pepper to taste. Continue to simmer until the beans are soft and beginning to break down and the ham meat comes off the bone easily when shredded with a fork, about 1 hour.

Remove the ham hock pieces. When they are cool enough to handle, remove the meat from the bones. Dice the meat and return it to the pot. Taste and adjust the seasonings. Ladle the soup into warmed bowls and garnish with parsley.

**Substitution Note:** Any white bean that will break down and become creamy will work nicely here. Try marrow beans, or if you don't have heirlooms, go with classic navy beans.

# SWEDISH BROWN BEAN
## SOUP

*Serves 4*

½ **POUND SWEDISH BROWN BEANS**, soaked (page 21)

6 **SLICES HIGH-QUALITY BACON**, diced

3 **CUPS SLICED GREEN CABBAGE**

2 **TABLESPOONS CIDER VINEGAR**

**PINCH PLUS 1 TEASPOON SALT**

1 **TABLESPOON MOLASSES**

1 **TABLESPOON BROWN SUGAR**

1 **TABLESPOON GRATED LEMON ZEST**

2 **TABLESPOONS CHOPPED FRESH FLAT-LEAF PARSLEY**

*I grew up in California, and a simple pot of beans or Mexican-style refried beans were more common than traditional East Coast baked beans. I don't think I ever had baked beans until I was a teenager. This soup has a lot of the same flavors without so much fussing. It was inspired by a recipe from chef Deborah Madison. Swedish brown beans are one of the most requested heirloom varieties at the farmers' market, especially once the winter settles in.*

Put the beans and their soaking liquid in a soup pot and add enough cold water to cover by 1 inch. Bring to a boil, reduce the heat to low, and simmer gently until beans are about half done, 45 minutes to 1 hour.

Meanwhile, in a large, heavy skillet over medium heat, sauté the bacon until the fat is nearly rendered but the bacon has not begun to brown, about 8 minutes. Pour off all but 1 tablespoonful of the fat, leaving the bacon in the pan. Add the cabbage, and toss with the bacon fat to coat. Cook the cabbage over medium heat until wilted and beginning to brown, 6 to 8 minutes. Add the cider vinegar and a pinch of salt. Stir and toss for 1 to 2 minutes. Add the cabbage, bacon, molasses, brown sugar, and 1 teaspoon salt to the beans. Cook, uncovered, over medium heat, stirring occasionally, until the beans are tender, about 1 hour. Add water if the soup is too thick.

In a small bowl, combine the lemon zest and parsley. Ladle the soup into warmed bowls and garnish with the lemon zest mixture.

**Substitution Note:** You could try Good Mother Stallard beans or perhaps *mayacoba* beans.

# GOOD MOTHER STALLARD BEAN AND BARLEY SOUP

*Serves 6*

½ **POUND GOOD MOTHER STALLARD BEANS**, soaked (page 21) and drained

**2 LEEKS**, sliced

¾ **CUP HULLED BARLEY**

**1 TEASPOON SALT**, plus more to taste

½ **SMALL HEAD SAVOY** or **REGULAR GREEN CABBAGE**, shredded

**1 LARGE CARROT**, peeled and cut into ¼-inch dice

**FRESHLY GROUND PEPPER**

¼ **CUP CHOPPED FRESH DILL**

**SOUR CREAM** for garnishing

*This soup is based on the traditional hearty and nourishing eastern European barley soups. Those porridges were very austere, but this version is embellished with cabbage.*

Cook the beans with 2 sliced leeks for the mirepoix as directed on page 23 until half cooked, about 30 to 60 minutes. Add the barley and 1 teaspoon salt and cook over medium heat for 30 minutes. Add the cabbage and stir to wilt. Add the carrot and season to taste with salt and pepper. Add water if needed to keep the ingredients submerged. Cover and simmer over medium-low heat until the flavors are blended and the vegetables, beans, and barley are tender, 45 to 60 minutes. Add water if the soup is too thick. Remove from the heat and stir in the dill. Ladle into warmed bowls and garnish with sour cream.

**Substitution Note:** Use more readily available cranberry beans instead of the Good Mother Stallard beans.

# SOMEWHAT
# TARASCAN
# BEAN
# SOUP

*Serves 4*

1 POUND PLUM TOMATOES, halved

3 TABLESPOONS EXTRA-VIRGIN OLIVE OIL

½ WHITE ONION, thinly sliced

2 GARLIC CLOVES, minced

4 CUPS COOKED OCTOBER or OTHER CRANBERRY BEANS in their broth (page 23)

3 TO 4 CUPS HOMEMADE (see page 130) or PURCHASED CHICKEN BROTH

1 TEASPOON DRIED MEXICAN OREGANO

SALT

*In the beautiful little town of Pátzcuaro, Mexico, one of the local specialties is Tarascan soup, most likely named for the local indigenous people. Of the several variations, the best is generally a mixture of tomatoes, chicken stock, and puréed beans. One day I made the soup with a cranberry bean rather than the more traditional* bayo *and was just knocked out. Cranberry beans are rich and velvety, and the texture of the puréed soup, topped with crunchy fried tortilla strips and chiles, was addictive. I later had the soup in Pátzcuaro, made with a proper* bayo *bean, and I much preferred my own version with a cranberry bean!*

Line a large, heavy skillet or *comal* with aluminum foil. Set over medium-high heat. Put the tomatoes cut side down in the pan and cook, turning occasionally with tongs, until blackened and soft, 10 to 15 minutes. Remove the tomatoes from the pan and chop. Set aside.

Remove the foil from the skillet or *comal* and discard. In the skillet or *comal* over medium-high heat, warm the olive oil. Add the onion, garlic, and tomatoes and sauté until soft, about 10 minutes. Let cool slightly. Put the vegetables in a blender and blend until smooth. Transfer to a soup pot.

Purée the beans and their broth in the blender, adding some of the chicken broth if necessary to keep the blades moving. Transfer to the pot. Bring to a simmer and cook, stirring occasionally, for about 5 minutes.

**SAFFLOWER** or **GRAPESEED OIL** for frying

**2 DAY-OLD CORN TORTILLAS**, cut into thin strips

**2 ANCHO CHILES**, seeded and cut into narrow strips

**½ CUP *QUESO FRESCO*** or other mild, moist white cheese

**SOUR CREAM** for serving

**FRESH CILANTRO LEAVES** for serving

Add the chicken broth and oregano and season with salt. Cook for 10 minutes to allow the flavors to blend.

Meanwhile, pour the safflower oil to a depth of about ½ inch into a small, heavy skillet. Set over medium-high heat and heat the oil until it is shimmering. Fry the tortilla strips, turning with tongs, until crisp and medium brown, 2 to 3 minutes. Remove to paper towels to drain. Fry the ancho chile strips until they puff up and emit a spicy aroma, 2 or 3 seconds. Remove quickly as they can become bitter if overcooked.

Put a little cheese, a few chile strips, and some tortilla strips in each warmed bowl. Pour in the hot soup. Pass the sour cream and cilantro at the table for garnishing the soup.

# CARIBBEAN BLACK BEAN SOUP
## WITH ROASTED GARLIC AND TOMATOES

*Serves 4*

---

**6 GARLIC CLOVES**, unpeeled

**2 TABLESPOONS EXTRA-VIRGIN OLIVE OIL**, plus more for drizzling

**4 WHOLE FRESH** or **CANNED PLUM TOMATOES**, with juice

**SALT**

½ **POUND BLACK VALENTINE** or **BLACK BEANS**, cooked (page 23), with reserved broth

½ **MEDIUM YELLOW** or **WHITE ONION**, chopped

**1 JALAPEÑO CHILE**, chopped

**1 MEDIUM CARROT**, peeled and chopped

**1½ TEASPOONS CUMIN SEEDS**, toasted and ground (page 29)

**1 TEASPOON DRIED OREGANO**

½ **TEASPOON CAYENNE PEPPER**

**2 CUPS CHICKEN** or **VEGETABLE BROTH**

**FRESHLY GROUND PEPPER**

**SOUR CREAM** for garnishing

**1 AVOCADO**, pitted, peeled, and sliced, for garnishing

**FRESH CILANTRO LEAVES** for garnishing

*A great, substantial bean soup like this one makes you realize how easy it is to enjoy meat-free meals. I could live on bowls of soup just like this. The secret to the rich flavor is in the caramelizing of the aromatic vegetables and the deep roasting of the garlic and tomatoes.*

Preheat the oven to 400°F.

Put the garlic cloves on a sheet of aluminum foil, drizzle with olive oil, and wrap in the foil. Put the tomatoes in a baking dish. If using fresh tomatoes, cut them in half and put them cut side down in the dish. Season with salt, and drizzle with olive oil. Roast the tomatoes and garlic until soft, fragrant, and brown, about 20 minutes.

Meanwhile, put the beans and their broth in a soup pot and warm over low heat.

In a medium, heavy skillet over medium-high heat, warm the 2 tablespoons olive oil. Add the onion, chile, and carrot and sauté until fragrant and beginning to caramelize, about 10 minutes. Add the cooked vegetables, cumin, oregano, cayenne, and chicken broth to the beans.

Peel the roasted garlic cloves. Chop the garlic cloves and tomatoes coarsely. Add the garlic and roasted tomatoes to the beans. Season with salt and pepper to taste. Bring to a simmer over medium-low heat and cook until the vegetables are soft and the flavors are blended, about 15 minutes.

Let the soup cool slightly. Transfer about half the soup to a blender. Blend until smooth. Return the soup to the pot, stir, and adjust the seasonings.

Ladle the soup into warmed bowls and garnish with sour cream, avocado slices, and cilantro.

# POSOLE WITH
# EYE OF THE GOAT BEANS
## AND CHICKEN

*Serves 4*

**1 MEDIUM WHITE ONION**, quartered

**⅔ CUP POSOLE**, soaked for several hours or overnight and drained

**SALT**

**3 DRIED NEW MEXICO CHILES**

**BOILING WATER**

**2 TABLESPOONS MILD OLIVE OIL** or **SUNFLOWER OIL**

**2 GARLIC CLOVES**, finely chopped

**1½ TEASPOONS DRIED MEXICAN OREGANO**

**4 CUPS HOMEMADE** (see page 130) or **PURCHASED CHICKEN BROTH**

**4 WHOLE FRESH** or **CANNED PLUM TOMATOES**, chopped and drained

**2 CUPS DRAINED, COOKED EYE OF THE GOAT BEANS** (page 23)

**1½ CUPS SHREDDED COOKED CHICKEN** (see page 130)

**FRESHLY GROUND PEPPER**

**CORN TORTILLAS**, warmed, for serving

**1 AVOCADO**, pitted, peeled, and diced, for serving

**1 LIME**, quartered for serving

**½ CUP CILANTRO LEAVES** for serving

*Beans and corn work so well as neighbors in the soil that a reunion on your stove is a good idea. I grew up thinking hominy was waxy and squeaky and not something I particularly liked. Of course, I was eating the canned version. Making posole from scratch is more work, but the payoff is well worth it. Prepared hominy or dry posole already has the skin removed so you just have to soak and simmer it. This dish comes together quickly if you have leftover cooked chicken and you soak and cook both the beans and the posole the day before you plan on making it. You can use leftover chicken or purchased rotisserie chicken, or follow the directions on page 130 for poaching the chicken.*

Roughly chop 1 onion quarter. In a medium saucepan, combine the posole and the chopped onion quarter, and add enough water to cover by 2 inches. Bring to a simmer over medium-low heat, cover, and cook until the posole is tender, about 3 hours. Season with salt toward the end of cooking and add water as needed to keep the posole submerged.

Slit the chiles and remove the seeds and stems. Heat a small, heavy skillet over medium-high heat and toast the chiles until they puff slightly and begin to emit a spicy fragrance, about 15 seconds per side. Watch them carefully so you don't burn them or they'll turn bitter. Place the chiles in a small bowl and pour boiling water over them to cover. Let soak for 20 to 30 minutes.

In a blender, purée the chiles with enough of their soaking water to make a purée about the consistency of buttermilk.

*continued*-

## POSOLE WITH
# EYE OF THE GOAT BEANS
## AND CHICKEN

*-continued*

Cut 2 onion quarters into thin slices. In a soup pot over medium heat, warm the oil. Add the sliced onion quarters and garlic and sauté until soft and fragrant, 3 to 4 minutes. Add the oregano, chicken broth, chili purée, and tomatoes. Add the posole with 1 cup of its cooking liquid. Bring the mixture to a boil and add a little salt if needed. Add the beans and simmer for 20 minutes to allow the flavors to blend. Add the chicken and stir to warm through. Season with salt and pepper.

Cut the remaining onion quarter into a small dice. Ladle the soup into warmed deep bowls. Pass the onion, tortillas, avocado, lime, and cilantro at the table.

**Substitution Note:** Any pintolike bean will work nicely here, such as Rio Zape for a deeper, richer soup, or Anasazi or *flor de junio*.

## *Posole*

The process of making *nixtamalized* corn for posole is the same as for making corn masa (page 39). Whole kernels of dried corn are soaked in lime overnight, and then the skins are gently rubbed off and the corn is rinsed. In the American Southwest, this treated corn is dried again. The resulting product is called posole or prepared hominy, which only needs to soak and simmer. I've never seen this product in Mexico, where the corn is sold untreated or canned.

The canned corn, also called hominy, has a rubbery, gummy texture and I can't recommend it. My Mexican friends will disagree but I think American posole is a better product. The kernels are finer and are easier to use.

In the United States, both the kernels and the dish are called posole, with an *s*. In Mexico, only the finished dish is called pozole, more often than not with a *z*.

# BEAN STEW
## WITH HERB PESTO

*Serves 4*

2 THYME SPRIGS

2 FRESH FLAT-LEAF PARSLEY SPRIGS

1 BAY LEAF

2 TABLESPOONS EXTRA-VIRGIN OLIVE OIL

½ **MEDIUM CARROT**, peeled and cut into 2 or 3 pieces

½ **CELERY STALK**, cut into 2 or 3 pieces

½ **MEDIUM YELLOW ONION**, quartered

¼ **MEDIUM FENNEL BULB**

ONE 3- TO 4-OUNCE PIECE OF PANCETTA

1 POUND YELLOW EYE, VAQUERO, MARROW, or **WHITE RUNNER BEANS**, soaked (page 21) and drained

3 CUPS HOMEMADE (see page 130) or **PURCHASED CHICKEN BROTH**

SALT AND FRESHLY GROUND PEPPER

*Almost weekly I get a call from the famous Blue Hill Restaurant at Stone Barns in New York. Chef and owner Dan Barber or chef and kitchen director Adam Kaye will want to discuss beans, quinoa, popcorn, or whatever else they might have on their minds. I can talk beans for hours, and Dan and Adam are either really interested or too polite to tell me to be quiet. Stone Barns not only houses the restaurant but is also a working farm and an educational center. Most of the greens and herbs used in this recipe would typically come straight off the farm and go into Chef Barber's kitchen. This recipe provides extra pesto, which is wonderful stirred into soups, pasta dishes, or bean salads.*

Put the thyme sprigs, parsley sprigs, and bay leaf on a piece of cheesecloth, gather the corners, and tie the bundle securely.

In a soup pot over medium heat, warm the olive oil. Add the carrot, celery, onion, fennel, and pancetta and sauté until the vegetables begin to soften and caramelize, about 10 minutes. Add the beans, cheesecloth bundle, chicken broth, and enough cold water to cover by 1 inch. Bring to a simmer and season with salt and pepper. Cook uncovered until the beans are just tender, about 1½ hours.

Transfer the beans and their broth to a large bowl and let cool. Remove the vegetables, pancetta, and cheesecloth bundle, and discard. Drain the beans, reserving the broth.

*continued -*

# BEAN STEW
## WITH HERB PESTO

*-continued*

## PESTO

**4 CORNICHONS**

**2 TEASPOONS CAPERS**

**¾ TABLESPOON DIJON MUSTARD**

**½ TEASPOON FINELY CHOPPED GARLIC**

**1 SOFT-COOKED EGG**

**1 OIL-PACKED ANCHOVY FILLET**

**1 CUP EXTRA-VIRGIN OLIVE OIL**

**2 CUPS ARUGULA LEAVES**, roughly chopped

**2 CUPS SPINACH LEAVES**, roughly chopped

**1 CUP FRESH CHERVIL LEAVES**, roughly chopped

**½ CUP FRESH TARRAGON LEAVES**

**SALT AND FRESHLY GROUND PEPPER**

**1 TABLESPOON FRESH TARRAGON LEAVES** for garnishing

**1 TABLESPOON CHOPPED PARSLEY** for garnishing

**Make the pesto:** Put the cornichons, capers, mustard, garlic, egg, and anchovy in a blender. With the motor running, slowly add the oil until it is completely incorporated. Add the arugula, spinach, chervil, and ½ cup tarragon. Purée until smooth. Season to taste with salt and pepper.

Put the beans and the reserved broth in a medium saucepan and warm gently over medium heat. Add about 1 cup of the pesto and stir to incorporate, making sure not to let the stew boil. Taste and adjust the seasonings. Ladle the stew into warmed bowls and garnish with the tarragon and parsley.

NEW WORLD

# TEPARY BEAN AND SUMMER VEGETABLE STEW

*Serves 4*

---

½ **POUND TEPARY BEANS**, cooked (page 23), in their broth

1 **MEDIUM RED** or **YELLOW BELL PEPPER**, roasted (page 29) and cut into strips

2 **SMALL ZUCCHINI**, cut in half lengthwise and then on the diagonal into ¼-inch slices

**ABOUT ⅓ POUND GREEN BEANS**, trimmed and cut into 1-inch lengths

4 **OR 5 PLUM TOMATOES**, coarsely chopped

2 **TEASPOONS CHOPPED FRESH THYME LEAVES**

**SALT AND FRESHLY GROUND PEPPER**

3 **TO 4 OUNCES FETA CHEESE**, crumbled, for garnishing

*Tepary beans are a beautiful example of why I focus on foods indigenous to the Americas. They are a superfood, higher in protein and fiber than other beans; the plants require little water to grow (a fact too often neglected in a drought-prone state like California), have few natural enemies, and are prolific. But the beans are virtually a secret to most Americans.*

*Teparies cook up firm and dense, and have an appealing sweetness that pairs well with summer vegetables. The vegetables in this stew are abundant and of high quality in summer, and each one also happens to originate in the New World. This hearty, one-dish stew can easily be adapted to the season. Try squash, fennel, and greens in winter, and asparagus and snap peas in spring. The last-minute addition of briny feta cuts the richness of the stew.*

In a soup pot over low heat, gently warm the beans, stirring occasionally. Add a little water if they appear too thick, starting with about ½ cup. Don't thin the beans too much, as the vegetables will release their liquid.

Add the bell pepper, zucchini, green beans, tomatoes, and thyme. Season to taste with salt and pepper. Simmer gently, stirring occasionally, until the vegetables are tender, about 20 minutes.

Ladle the stew into warmed shallow bowls and garnish with the crumbled feta.

**Substitution Note:** Teparies are unique and really have no substitute. The best places to find them are through online sources. Any of the pintolike beans will make a fine, but different, stew.

RANCHO GORDO

# RED CHILI CON CARNE

*Serves 4 to 5*

¼ CUP EXTRA-VIRGIN OLIVE OIL

2½ POUNDS CHUCK ROAST, cut into ½- to 1-inch cubes

2 MEDIUM WHITE ONIONS, roughly chopped

4 TO 6 GARLIC CLOVES

1 TABLESPOON DRIED MEXICAN OREGANO

½ CUP GOOD-QUALITY NEW MEXICO CHILE POWDER

1 TEASPOON CUMIN SEEDS, toasted and ground (page 29)

SALT

3 CUPS WATER

1 BOTTLE DARK BEER

1 CUP DRAINED, COOKED GOOD MOTHER STALLARD or PINTO BEANS (page 23)

1 TABLESPOON MASA HARINA (optional)

CHOPPED WHITE ONION for serving

CHOPPED FRESH CILANTRO for serving

*Among chili aficionados, your answer to the question "beans or no beans?" can earn you disdain or respect. I love beans in my chili, but I dislike the thick, stodgy mess made from mostly beans and called "chili con carne." The star should be the chiles, from pods or from chiles ground to a powder. Even the meat takes a back seat, as do the beans.*

*A note on the spelling: The pods are called chiles. The dish is called chili. When you see chile powder, you should expect 100 percent ground chiles. If it's called chili powder, there's a good chance it has added spices and herbs.*

In a soup pot or Dutch oven over medium-high heat, warm the olive oil. Working in batches, add the meat and cook, turning with tongs, until evenly browned. Remove from the pot and set aside. Reduce the heat to medium, add the roughly chopped onions and garlic, and sauté until soft and fragrant, about 10 minutes. Add the oregano, chile powder, cumin, and salt to taste. Cook the spices, stirring, for 1 to 2 minutes. Gradually stir in the water and beer. Bring to a boil, reduce heat to low, return the meat to the pot, cover, and simmer slowly, stirring occasionally, until the meat is tender, about 2 hours.

Add the beans and simmer for 10 minutes. At this point, the texture will be somewhat soupy. If you'd like a thicker chili, dissolve the masa harina in ½ cup water, stirring well to eliminate lumps. Slowly drizzle the liquid into the chili while stirring. Simmer over low heat for 15 minutes or so. Taste and adjust the salt. Ladle the chili into warmed bowls and pass the chopped onion and cilantro at the table.

# ANASAZI COWBOY CHILI
## WITH BUFFALO AND NOPALES

*Serves 6*

**1 POUND ANASAZI BEANS**, soaked (page 21)

**1½ MEDIUM WHITE ONIONS**, chopped

**6 GARLIC CLOVES**, finely chopped

**SALT**

**2 TABLESPOONS EXTRA-VIRGIN OLIVE OIL**

**1 POUND GROUND BUFFALO**

**1 JALAPEÑO CHILE**, finely chopped

**2 TEASPOONS CUMIN SEEDS**, toasted and ground (page 29)

**1 TEASPOON DRIED MEXICAN OREGANO**

**1 TEASPOON GOOD-QUALITY HOT CHILE POWDER** such as chipotle

**ONE 14.5-OUNCE CAN CRUSHED TOMATOES**

**1 CUP LAGER BEER**

**FRESHLY GROUND PEPPER**

**2 TABLESPOONS MASA HARINA** (optional)

**2 NOPALES PADDLES (ABOUT ¾ POUND)**, prepared and cooked (page 29)

*At farmers' markets, whenever things get slow, I take out a cactus paddle and start removing the spines with a sharp knife. Nothing seems to draw a bigger crowd. Many people are intimidated by nopales, but they are not difficult to prepare. Their unique flavor can be described as being between aspara-gus and green pepper. If nopales are unavailable, they can be left out. But don't give up too easily. Check your local Mexican or South American markets, or ask your supermarket produce manager to get some for you. The masa harina is a traditional but optional thickener. If you want a thinner chili, skip it altogether. I like the flavor.*

Put the beans in a large pot with their soaking water and enough cold water to cover the beans by 1 inch. Bring to a boil. Add one-third of the onions and half of the chopped garlic. Reduce the heat to low and simmer, partially covered, until the beans are nearly done, about 1 hour. Season with salt.

Meanwhile, in a soup pot or Dutch oven over medium-high heat, warm the oil. Add the meat, season with salt, and cook, stirring, until the meat loses all of its pink color and begins to brown. Remove with a slotted spoon and set aside. Pour off most of the fat. Add the remaining onions and garlic and the chile, and sauté until soft, about 10 minutes, scraping up any browned bits clinging to the bottom of the pot. Add the cumin, oregano, chile powder, tomatoes with their juice, and beer and return the meat to the pot. Add the beans and their broth. Bring to a boil, reduce the heat to low, cover, and simmer gently until the flavors are blended and the beans are tender, about 30 minutes. Taste and adjust the sea-sonings, adding salt and pepper and more chile powder if needed.

*continued-*

# ANASAZI
# COWBOY CHILI
## WITH BUFFALO AND NOPALES

*-continued*

### FOR SERVING

**SOUR CREAM**

**GRATED CHEDDAR CHEESE**

**SLICED GREEN ONIONS**, white and pale green parts

**CHOPPED FRESH CILANTRO**

If you'd like a thicker chili, dissolve the masa harina in ½ cup water, stirring well to eliminate lumps. Stir the paste into the chili, add the nopales, adjust the seasonings, and cook for 10 minutes. Ladle the chili into warmed bowls. Pass the sour cream, grated cheese, green onions, and cilantro at the table.

**Substitution Note:** Any of the pinto beans will work nicely in this chili, as will Vallarta, yellow Indian woman, or black beans.

# CHILI VERDE WITH ANASAZI BEANS

*Serves 8 to 10*

8 TOMATILLOS, husks removed

2 TABLESPOONS EXTRA-VIRGIN OLIVE OIL or SUNFLOWER OIL

½ MEDIUM WHITE ONION, chopped

3 GARLIC CLOVES, finely chopped

1 TEASPOON CUMIN SEEDS, toasted and finely ground (page 29)

ONE 3-POUND BONELESS PORK SHOULDER, trimmed of excess fat and cut into ¾-inch cubes

8 POBLANO CHILES, roasted (page 29) and cut into strips

½ CUP FRESH CILANTRO LEAVES, plus 2 tablespoons chopped for serving

1 TEASPOON DRIED MEXICAN OREGANO

1 TO 2 CUPS HOMEMADE (see page 130) or PURCHASED CHICKEN BROTH

SALT AND FRESHLY GROUND PEPPER

2 CUPS COOKED ANASAZI BEANS in their broth (page 23)

*Chili verde is simply a green chile stew. Of the countless variations, the best ones use a good mix of poblano chiles and tomatillos. Tomatillos, like potatoes and tomatoes, are in the nightshade family. They're easy to grow, and it's likely you need to plant them just once and you'll have naturalized volunteer plants ever after. The sweetest are the small purple ones, called* milperos, *that grow among the corn stalks. If you come across some, throw them into your soil and see what happens next spring. This chili feeds a crowd. Serve it with corn tortillas, rice, and even coleslaw.*

Bring a medium saucepan of water to a boil. Add the tomatillos and cook until soft, about 5 minutes. Drain and rinse under cold running water, then chop.

In a soup pot or Dutch oven over medium heat, warm the oil. Add the onion, garlic, and cumin and sauté until the vegetables are soft and fragrant, about 10 minutes. Add the pork, chiles, tomatillos, cilantro leaves, and oregano. Pour in enough chicken broth to cover the pork. Season with salt and pepper and bring to a simmer. Cover and cook until the pork is tender and shreds easily with a fork, 1 to 1½ hours. Add the beans and cook for 30 minutes. Ladle the chili into warmed bowls and garnish with the chopped cilantro.

**Substitution Note:** Any pintolike bean will work here. Try eye of the tiger or eye of the goat.

# WHITE CHILI
## WITH TURKEY AND GREEN CHILES

*Serves 6 to 8*

**12 TOMATILLOS**, husks removed

**2 TABLESPOONS EXTRA-VIRGIN OLIVE OIL**

**2 POUNDS GROUND TURKEY**

**1 MEDIUM YELLOW ONION**, chopped

**3 GARLIC CLOVES**, finely chopped

**3 POBLANO CHILES**, roasted (page 29) and diced

**3 TO 5 SERRANO CHILES**, seeded and finely sliced

**2 TEASPOONS CORIANDER SEEDS**, toasted and ground (page 29)

**3 TABLESPOONS CUMIN SEEDS**, toasted and ground (page 29)

**1 TEASPOON CAYENNE PEPPER**

**1 TEASPOON DRIED MEXICAN OREGANO**

**1 BAY LEAF**

**SALT AND FRESHLY GROUND PEPPER**

**1 CUP HOMEMADE** (see page 130) or **PURCHASED CHICKEN BROTH**, or more if needed

**3 CUPS COOKED *CELLINI* BEANS** in their broth (page 23)

### FOR SERVING

**CHOPPED FRESH CILANTRO**

**SLICED GREEN ONIONS**, white and pale green parts

**CRUMBLED *QUESO FRESCO***

**SOUR CREAM**

**LIME WEDGES**

*"White chili" always struck me as one of those awful potluck dishes I've lived my life trying to avoid. Of course, I'd never tasted it, but why let that little fact stop me from judging it? The way people would go on about a white bean and chicken dish always made me feel as if they were too faint of heart for real chili. Well, guess what? White chili is delicious, but has got almost nothing to do with "chili." As the dish is so rich, I think a squeeze of lime at the end makes it perfect.*

Bring a medium saucepan of water to a boil. Add the tomatillos and cook until soft, about 5 minutes. Drain and rinse under cold running water, then chop.

In a soup pot or Dutch oven over medium heat, warm the olive oil. Add the turkey and cook, breaking it up with a wooden spoon, until it has lost its pink color. Remove with a slotted spoon and set aside.

Add the onion and garlic and cook until soft and fragrant, about 10 minutes. Return the turkey to the pot and add the poblano and serrano chiles, coriander, cumin, cayenne, oregano, and bay leaf. Season with salt and pepper. Add the tomatillos and 1 cup chicken broth. Bring to a simmer, reduce the heat to low, and cook, uncovered, until the flavors blend, about 45 minutes. Gently stir in the beans, adjust the seasonings, add more chicken broth if a thinner chili is desired, and cook for about 30 minutes to blend the flavors.

Ladle the chili into warmed bowls and pass the cilantro, green onions, *queso fresco*, sour cream, and lime wedges at the table.

**Substitution Note:** Any of the white beans such as marrow or runner cannellini will work here. For something different, you might try yellow eye or European soldier beans.

# YELLOW EYE CHOWDER

## WITH SMOKED CHICKEN, SWEET POTATOES, AND SAGE

*Serves 6 to 8*

2 TO 3 TABLESPOONS EXTRA-VIRGIN OLIVE OIL

1 LARGE YELLOW ONION, finely chopped

2 CELERY STALKS, finely chopped

3 CLOVES GARLIC, finely chopped

1 POUND YELLOW EYE or BALCK CALYPSO BEANS, soaked (page 21)

2 SMALL GARNET SWEET POTATOES, cut into ⅓-inch dice

½ POUND SMOKED CHICKEN, shredded

2 TO 3 TABLESPOONS CHOPPED FRESH SAGE

SALT AND FRESHLY GROUND PEPPER

CHOPPED FRESH FLAT-LEAF PARSLEY for garnishing

*Yellow eye beans have a neutral yet earthy flavor and a crumbly texture when cooked, making them naturals for chowder. Sage has a warming flavor that pairs beautifully with any sweet vegetable. Add smoky chicken and you have a hearty soup that is perfect for cold-weather eating. Serve this soup with your favorite artisan bread and a salad of beets, oranges, and spinach for a winter meal.*

In a soup pot over medium heat, warm the olive oil. Add the onion, celery, and garlic and sauté until soft and fragrant, about 10 minutes. Add the beans and their soaking water, and enough additional cold water to cover the beans by 1 inch. Bring to a boil, cover partially, and simmer until the beans are just starting to soften but are still fairly firm, about 1 hour.

Add the sweet potatoes, chicken, sage, and salt and pepper to taste. Bring to a gentle simmer and cook, stirring occasionally, until the beans are tender but not falling apart, about 20 minutes. Ladle the chowder into warmed bowls and garnish with chopped parsley.

**Substitution Note:** You can use Jacob's cattle or any of the white beans for this chowder.

## Turkey in the New World

Along with beans, peppers, chiles, potatoes, squash, and corn, turkeys were once exclusive to the Americas. Before the conquest, they ranged from Ontario to the southeastern United States, and throughout the Southwest, Mexico, and Central America.

Pueblo Indians, Aztecs, and Mayans were the first to domesticate the bird for food, feathers, and ritual sacrifice. They did the world a favor because it was this domesticated turkey that traveled with the conquistadores in the sixteenth century back to the Old World, where it found a place of importance on European tables.

The turkey's importance in the New World has never waned. In addition to its enduring status as a favorite harvest centerpiece, turkey is still eaten throughout Mexico on festival days. One of the great national dishes of Mexico, *mole poblano*, brings the New World and Old World together with its beguiling blend of chiles, spices, nuts, and seeds.

*chapter*

# 3

# SALADS

# THREE-BEAN SALAD
## WITH ROASTED TOMATOES AND PANCETTA

*Serves 4 to 6*

ONE 14-OUNCE CAN WHOLE PLUM TOMATOES, drained

1 TABLESPOON EXTRA-VIRGIN OLIVE OIL

SALT

¼ POUND PANCETTA, cut into ¼-inch dice

1½ CUPS EACH WELL-DRAINED, COOKED YELLOW INDIAN WOMAN, *CELLINI*, AND RED NIGHTFALL BEANS, (page 23), warmed slightly

3 CELERY STALKS, cut in half lengthwise and then on the diagonal into ¼-inch-thick slices

1 SMALL SWEET ONION, cut into quarters and then into thin slices

¼ CUP CHOPPED FRESH FLAT-LEAF PARSLEY

BUTTER LETTUCE or ESCAROLE, shredded, for serving

FRESHLY GROUND PEPPER

*Once I was in a Mexican market and spotted a large basket of beans. This basket was almost unbelievable. Each bean was a different color and shape! I'm always on the lookout for new bean varieties, and in the basket I saw a bean that I was sure was going to be my greatest discovery. The bean was called* revueltos. *The name sounded exotic and romantic until I remembered that scrambled eggs are called* revueltos. *That sinking feeling came over me as I realized the name of the bean wasn't* revueltos. *These were the bottom-of-the-bin beans all scrambled together. At least I had a good laugh. Normally I don't mix beans when I cook them. I prefer their flavors and textures pure, but cooking them separately and serving them in a salad makes good sense. The pairing of beans and pancetta is easy to like.*

Preheat the oven to 400°F. Cover a baking sheet with parchment paper. Put the tomatoes on the prepared sheet. Drizzle with the olive oil and sprinkle with salt. Roast until they are fragrant and beginning to brown and caramelize, about 20 minutes.

Meanwhile, in a small, heavy skillet, sauté the pancetta until golden, 8 to 10 minutes. Remove to paper towels to drain.

Chop the tomatoes coarsely. Put them in a large salad bowl. Add the pancetta, beans, celery, onion, and parsley.

*continued-*

# THREE-BEAN SALAD
## WITH ROASTED TOMATOES AND PANCETTA

*-continued*

## DRESSING

**2 GARLIC CLOVES**, finely chopped

**¼ TEASPOON DRIED OREGANO**

**¼ TEASPOON DRIED THYME**

**1 TEASPOON DIJON MUSTARD**

**3 TABLESPOONS RED WINE VINEGAR**

**½ CUP EXTRA-VIRGIN OLIVE OIL**

**SALT AND FRESHLY GROUND PEPPER**

**Make the dressing:** In a small bowl, whisk together the garlic, oregano, thyme, mustard, and vinegar. Slowly drizzle in the olive oil, whisking continually until the dressing comes together. Season to taste with salt and pepper.

Pour in the dressing, toss well, and season with salt and pepper. Serve on a bed of lettuce.

**Substitution Note:** Any bean that cooks up firmly and holds its shape is ideal for a bean salad: cranberry beans; sturdy beans like flageolet, *mayacoba*, yellow Indian woman, Vallarta, and Santa Maria *pinquito*; and runner beans like scarlet runners and cannellini. Making a salad like this is a good way to become familiar with the characteristics of different beans.

# YELLOW INDIAN WOMAN

## BEANS AND BULGUR WITH PRESERVED LEMONS

*Serves 4*

---

1 CUP BULGUR

2 CUPS BOILING WATER

2 CUPS WELL-DRAINED, COOKED YELLOW INDIAN WOMAN BEANS (page 23), warmed slightly

2 TABLESPOONS FINELY CHOPPED PRESERVED LEMONS (recipe follows)

⅓ CUP CHOPPED GREEN ONION, white and pale green parts

ABOUT 1 CUP CHOPPED FRESH FLAT-LEAF PARSLEY

---

### DRESSING

¼ CUP FRESH LEMON JUICE

3 GARLIC CLOVES, minced

2 TEASPOONS *HARISSA* PASTE

⅓ CUP EXTRA-VIRGIN OLIVE OIL

SALT AND FRESHLY GROUND PEPPER

---

### PRESERVED LEMONS

8 TO 10 ORGANIC LEMONS

ABOUT 1 CUP KOSHER SALT

JUICE OF 5 OR 6 LEMONS

---

*Once you start using preserved lemons, you'll want to use them often. They add an intense kick to almost any dish, and this recipe is no exception. It may remind you of tabbouleh, but it's a bean dish first and foremost and a delicious one at that.*

Put the bulgur in a medium heatproof bowl and add the boiling water. Let soak for 1 hour. With a fork, fluff the soaked bulgur. It should be light and moist, but not wet. If necessary, drain the bulgur and squeeze out the excess water with your hands. Alternatively, spread the bulgur on a baking sheet in a thin layer and dry in a 300°F oven for 10 minutes.

Put the bulgur, beans, preserved lemon, green onion, and parsley in a large salad bowl.

**Make the dressing:** In a small bowl, whisk together the lemon juice, garlic, and *harissa*. Slowly drizzle in the olive oil, whisking continually until the dressing comes together. Season to taste with salt and pepper.

Pour the dressing over the salad and toss. Taste and adjust the seasonings. Serve at room temperature.

**Preserved Lemon:** Wash and dry the lemons thoroughly and cut each into quarters. In a large glass or ceramic bowl, toss the lemons with ⅓ cup of the salt. Put 2 tablespoons salt in the bottom of a sterilized 1-quart canning jar. Tightly pack the lemon quarters into the jar, stopping now and then to add another layer of salt. As you pack the lemons, push down on them to release some of the juice. Pour in enough juice to cover the lemons. If you have only a metal lid, cover the top of the jar with heavy-duty plastic wrap before closing the lid. Let the jar sit at room temperature for 3 weeks, shaking well once each day. Make sure the lemons remain submerged in juice. Refrigerate the lemons. They will keep for about 1 year. Rinse the lemons before using both the pulp and the rinds.

**Substitution Note:** Any firm salad bean such as *mayacoba*, Vallarta, or *cellini* can replace the yellow Indian woman.

# ITALIAN MARROW BEANS
## WITH TUNA

*Serves 4*

ONE 5-OUNCE CAN BEST-QUALITY, OLIVE OIL–PACKED TUNA, drained slightly

½ MEDIUM SWEET ONION, very thinly sliced

1 CELERY STALK, cut in half lengthwise and then on the diagonal into ¼-inch-thick slices

⅓ CUP CHOPPED FRESH FLAT-LEAF PARSLEY

2½ CUPS WELL-DRAINED, COOKED MARROW BEANS (page 23), warmed slightly

3 TABLESPOONS EXTRA-VIRGIN OLIVE OIL

2 TEASPOONS RED WINE VINEGAR

SALT AND FRESHLY GROUND PEPPER

*Italian and Spanish cooks make variations of this dish, which at its base consists of beans, tuna, and oil. This is a dish where you can't skimp on any of the ingredients. Look for Italian, Spanish, or Portuguese tuna packed in olive oil. Add a small baguette and you have a great portable lunch. You could serve a green salad as well.*

Put the tuna in a salad bowl and break it up slightly with a fork. Add the onion, celery, parsley, and beans. Drizzle with the olive oil and vinegar. Season with salt and pepper and toss well. Taste and adjust the seasonings. Serve at room temperature within 2 hours.

**Substitution Note:** Runner cannellini or any other mild white bean will work here. Another option is flageolet.

# WHITE RUNNER BEAN
## SALAD

*Serves 4*

**DRESSING**

1 HARD-COOKED EGG

2 GARLIC CLOVES

2 OIL-PACKED ANCHOVY FILLETS

2 TABLESPOONS RED WINE VINEGAR

¼ CUP EXTRA-VIRGIN OLIVE OIL

SALT AND FRESHLY GROUND PEPPER

---

3 CUPS WELL-DRAINED, COOKED WHITE BEANS such as runner cannellini, *cellini*, or marrow (page 23), warmed slightly

½ MEDIUM RED BELL PEPPER, seeded and finely diced

¼ MEDIUM SWEET ONION, very thinly sliced

¼ CUP CHOPPED FRESH FLAT-LEAF PARSLEY

SALT AND FRESHLY GROUND PEPPER

TENDER YOUNG ESCAROLE LEAVES, shredded, for serving

*Many versions of the classic white bean salad exist in Italy. This one was inspired by a Marcella Hazan recipe. The hard-cooked egg becomes part of the dressing, providing a coating for the beans and vegetables.*

**Make the dressing:** Put the egg, garlic, and anchovies in a food processor. Process until smooth. Add the red wine vinegar and process. With the motor running, add the olive oil in a slow, steady stream, and process until the dressing comes together. Add salt and pepper to taste.

Put the beans in a salad bowl. Add the bell pepper, onion, and parsley. Pour in the dressing and toss. Taste and adjust the seasonings. Serve on a bed of shredded escarole.

# SCARLET RUNNER BEAN

## AND CRESS SALAD

*Serves 4*

### DRESSING

**2 GARLIC CLOVES**, chopped

**3 TABLESPOONS BALSAMIC VINEGAR**

**JUICE OF ½ LEMON**

**5 TABLESPOONS EXTRA-VIRGIN OLIVE OIL**

**SALT AND FRESHLY GROUND PEPPER**

**1½ CUPS WELL-DRAINED, COOKED SCARLET RUNNER BEANS** (page 23), warmed slightly

**1 BUNCH ANCHO CRESS** or **WATERCRESS**

**2 LARGE HANDFULS BABY ARUGULA**

**SALT AND FRESHLY GROUND PEPPER**

**PARMESAN CHEESE**, shaved with a vegetable peeler, for serving

*Scarlet runner beans are large, meaty, and versatile. They work in salads like this, but they can also replace meat in chilies and stews. Ancho cress, sometimes known as Persian cress, is very easy to grow if you can't find it at your farmers' market. Watercress is a delicious substitute.*

**Make the dressing:** In a small bowl, whisk together the garlic, vinegar, and lemon juice. Slowly drizzle in the olive oil, whisking continuously until the dressing comes together. Season to taste with salt and pepper.

In a salad bowl, toss together the beans, cress, and arugula. Season with salt and pepper. Pour in the dressing and toss well. Scatter Parmesan shavings over each serving or pass them at the table.

**Substitution Note:** Scarlet runners are unique, but any large, white, creamy runner bean will make a great version of this salad.

# RIO ZAPE BEANS AND SWEET POTATOES
## WITH FRIED SAGE AND PINE NUTS

*Serves 4*

2 MEDIUM GARNET SWEET POTATOES, peeled

1 TABLESPOON EXTRA-VIRGIN OLIVE OIL

½ TEASPOON SALT

2 TABLESPOONS PINE NUTS

¼ CUP SAFFLOWER or GRAPESEED OIL

16 TO 20 FRESH SAGE LEAVES

1 BUNCH WATERCRESS

1 CUP WELL-DRAINED, COOKED RIO ZAPE BEANS (page 23), warmed slightly

FRESHLY GROUND PEPPER

*The poor sweet potato seems to be served only around the holidays when it is humiliated by being made cloyingly sweet with a marshmallow necklace. Surely this fine tuber deserves better. In this salad, the dressing and sage help make the dish savory, while the pine nuts add an indulgent touch. Enjoy with pork chops or grilled sausage.*

Preheat the oven to 400°F.

Cut the sweet potatoes lengthwise into eighths, so you end up with wedges. Cut each wedge crosswise into bite-size triangles about ½ inch thick. Transfer to a medium bowl, add the olive oil and salt, and toss to coat. Spread in a single layer on a baking sheet. Roast, turning once with a spatula, until soft and beginning to caramelize, about 20 minutes.

Meanwhile, in a small, heavy skillet over low heat, toast the pine nuts, shaking the pan often and watching closely so the nuts don't burn, until golden and fragrant, 4 to 5 minutes. Transfer to a small bowl.

In a small, heavy skillet over medium-high heat, warm the safflower oil. Add the sage leaves, 4 at a time, and fry until they are crisp but remain bright green, 10 to 15 seconds. Remove to a paper towel to drain.

## DRESSING

**1 SMALL SHALLOT**, finely chopped

**1 TEASPOON DIJON MUSTARD**

**2 TABLESPOONS CIDER VINEGAR**

**¼ CUP EXTRA-VIRGIN OLIVE OIL**

**1 TABLESPOON CHOPPED FRESH FLAT-LEAF PARSLEY**

**1 TEASPOON CHOPPED FRESH CHERVIL**

**½ TEASPOON CHOPPED FRESH MARJORAM**

**SALT AND FRESHLY GROUND PEPPER**

**Make the dressing:** In a small bowl, whisk together the shallot, mustard, and vinegar. Slowly drizzle in the olive oil, whisking continually until the dressing comes together. Whisk in the parsley, chervil, and marjoram and season to taste with salt and pepper.

Put the watercress in a salad bowl, drizzle with a small amount of the dressing, and toss to coat. Season with salt and pepper. Divide the watercress among 4 serving plates. Toss the sweet potatoes in the dressing, reserving some for the beans. Place the potatoes on the watercress. Toss the beans in the remaining dressing, season with salt and pepper if needed, and spoon over the potatoes, making sure that the potatoes and beans are visible. Sprinkle with the pine nuts and garnish with the fried sage leaves.

**Substitution Note:** Try a cranberry variety or a scarlet runner for something different.

## Bean Salad Tips

We've all had them: the unfortunate bean salads. They come out of the deli case coated in a partially congealed sludge of oil. They show up at the potluck—all mushy beans and muddy flavors and not enough salt. Not only is it possible to make a good bean salad, but it is even possible to make a bean salad ahead of time whose flavors are bright and clean. Here are some basic rules.

**Warm the beans before dressing them.** Refrigerating the beans kills their flavor. As you're preparing the rest of the ingredients, warm the beans slightly on the stove top and toss them in the dressing while still slightly warm.

**Drain the beans well.** Although I love the pot liquor, it consists largely of water and can make the salad taste watery. Use a fine-mesh strainer and allow plenty of time for the liquid to drain. Don't rinse the beans.

**Season well with vinegar.** When making a dressing for greens, the ratio of oil to acid is usually 3 to 1. For beans, make it closer to 2 to 1. Beans are rich and require more vinegar or lemon juice than you're accustomed to using.

**Be generous with salt.** Bean salads need lots of salt because beans are porous and absorb the salt. If you're worried about sodium, cut down on salt somewhere else. If you've made the salad ahead and refrigerated it, you will need to salt it again before serving.

**Make the salad on the same day** no more than 2 hours before serving, if possible, to avoid refrigerating it.

**Serve the salad at room temperature.** If you need to chill a salad, never serve it straight from the refrigerator.

# WREN'S EGG BEANS AND GREEN BEANS

## WITH PECORINO ROMANO AND TOMATO-ANCHOVY VINAIGRETTE

*Serves 4*

### VINAIGRETTE

**2 OIL-PACKED ANCHOVY FILLETS**, or **1 SALT-PACKED ANCHOVY, FILLETED** (page 29)

**2 GARLIC CLOVES**

**SALT**

**2 FRESH** or **CANNED PLUM TOMATOES**, drained

**1 TEASPOON DIJON MUSTARD**

**2 TABLESPOONS RED WINE VINEGAR**

**$2/3$ CUP EXTRA-VIRGIN OLIVE OIL**

**FRESHLY GROUND PEPPER**

**1 POUND GREEN BEANS**, trimmed

**1½ CUPS WELL-DRAINED, COOKED WREN'S EGG BEANS** (page 23), warmed slightly

**$1/3$ CUP FINELY CHOPPED FRESH FLAT-LEAF PARSLEY**

**¼ POUND *PECORINO ROMANO* CHEESE**, cut into ¼-inch dice

**SALT AND FRESHLY GROUND PEPPER**

*Wren's egg beans are in the cranberry family and have an interesting characteristic. As they begin to cook, they give off a toasty corn aroma almost like that of fresh masa. I know many people who buy these little beans for the name and their resemblance to little wren's eggs. The vinaigrette makes more than you'll need, so use the remainder on full-flavored greens like arugula if you like.*

**Make the vinaigrette:** Put the anchovies in a mortar. Add the garlic and a pinch of salt and pound with a pestle to form a chunky paste. Transfer to a food processor. Add the tomatoes, mustard, and vinegar. Slowly drizzle in the olive oil, pulsing until the vinaigrette comes together. Season to taste with salt and pepper. Set aside. The vinaigrette can be made up to 3 days in advance.

Bring a large saucepan of salted water to a boil. Add the green beans and cook until crisp-tender, 3 to 4 minutes. Drain and pat dry. In a large salad bowl, toss the green beans with the wren's egg beans. Add the parsley and cheese and about $1/3$ cup of the vinaigrette, and toss. Season to taste with salt and pepper.

**Substitution Note:** Wren's egg beans are uncommon, but they're worth trying if you can find them. Otherwise, use another cranberry bean.

# FENNEL AND RADICCHIO WITH
# MAYACOBA BEANS,
## HAZELNUTS, AND BACON

*Serves 4*

2 MEDIUM FENNEL BULBS, trimmed

2 TABLESPOONS EXTRA-VIRGIN OLIVE OIL

SALT AND FRESHLY GROUND PEPPER

½ CUP HAZELNUTS

2 HEADS RADICCHIO DI TREVISO

1½ CUPS WELL-DRAINED, COOKED *MAYACOBA* or other firm, white beans (page 23), warmed slightly

6 SLICES HIGH-QUALITY BACON, fried until crisp and crumbled

PARMESAN CHEESE, shaved with a vegetable peeler, for serving

## DRESSING

½ SMALL SHALLOT, finely chopped

1 TEASPOON DIJON MUSTARD

1 TABLESPOON FRESH LEMON JUICE

1 TABLESPOON RED WINE VINEGAR

4 TABLESPOONS EXTRA-VIRGIN OLIVE OIL, or 2 tablespoons hazelnut oil and 2 tablespoons extra-virgin olive oil

SALT AND FRESHLY GROUND PEPPER

*Mayacobas are odd beans in that they have a thin skin and a thick, meaty center, almost the opposite of most beans. On their own, they have an old-fashioned comfort-food quality. Mayacobas hold their shape well and work great in salads.*

Preheat the oven to 300°F.

Cut each fennel bulb lengthwise into ⅓-inch-thick slices. Transfer to a medium bowl, drizzle with the olive oil, season with salt and pepper, and toss to coat. Working in batches if necessary, place the fennel in a single layer in a large, heavy skillet over medium-high heat. Cook the fennel, turning often, until golden brown and soft, 8 to 10 minutes. Coarsely chop the fennel and set aside.

Put the hazelnuts on a baking pan in a single layer and toast in the oven until fragrant, 8 to 10 minutes. Watch them closely so they don't burn. Remove from the oven and transfer to a small bowl. When the nuts are cool enough to handle, enclose them in a clean kitchen towel. Place your hands, palms down, on the towel and run them gently over the nuts in a rolling motion to loosen the papery skins. You may need to rub some of the nuts individually to remove the skins. Bits of remaining skin are acceptable. Crush them lightly in the same towel with the bottom of a heavy skillet to make them easier to chop. Coarsely chop the nuts.

Beginning at the narrow tip, cut each radicchio head crosswise into ⅓-inch-thick slices, discarding the tough core.

**Make the dressing:** In a small bowl, whisk together the shallot, mustard, lemon juice, and vinegar. Slowly drizzle in the olive oil, whisking continuously until the dressing comes together. Season to taste with salt and pepper.

Put the fennel and radicchio in a large salad bowl. Add the beans, bacon, and chopped hazelnuts. Pour in the dressing and toss gently. Season with salt and pepper and toss again. Scatter the Parmesan shavings over the salad and offer more shavings over individual servings.

# MAYACOBA BEAN SALAD
## WITH PESTO AND SHRIMP

*Serves 4*

**PESTO**

2 GARLIC CLOVES

ABOUT 2 CUPS LOOSELY PACKED FRESH BASIL LEAVES

½ TEASPOON SALT

⅓ CUP EXTRA-VIRGIN OLIVE OIL

FRESHLY GROUND PEPPER

1 BAY LEAF

¼ TEASPOON FENNEL SEEDS

¼ TEASPOON CORIANDER SEEDS

4 TO 5 PEPPERCORNS

1 GARLIC CLOVE, crushed

⅓ CUP DRY WHITE WINE

½ LEMON

½ TEASPOON SALT

½ POUND MEDIUM SHRIMP, peeled and deveined

2 CUPS WELL-DRAINED, COOKED *MAYACOBA* BEANS (page 23), warmed slightly

1 CUP HALVED CHERRY or GRAPE TOMATOES

SALT AND FRESHLY GROUND PEPPER

JUICE OF ½ LEMON

*Beans and seafood aren't one of the more obvious matches in the kitchen. It's a shame because the creaminess of the beans makes a rich seafood dish that's great with a crisp white wine like a Napa or Sonoma Sauvignon Blanc. The standard cheese and pine nuts are omitted from this pesto to keep the flavors pure.*

**Make the pesto:** Put the garlic, basil, and salt in a food processor. Pulse until chopped. With the motor running, slowly drizzle in the olive oil, and process until blended. Season to taste with pepper. Set aside.

Bring a small saucepan of water to a boil. Add the bay leaf, fennel and coriander seeds, peppercorns, garlic, wine, lemon half, and ½ teaspoon salt. Reduce the heat to low and simmer for 10 minutes. Add the shrimp, bring to a boil, and cook until the shrimp are opaque and firm, about 30 seconds. Drain well.

Put the beans and cherry tomatoes in a large salad bowl. Add the shrimp and toss gently. Pour the pesto over the salad. Toss and season with salt and pepper and the lemon juice. Serve warm or at room temperature.

**Substitution Note:** *Mayacoba* beans are white beans, so use cannellini, *cellini*, or marrow beans in their place. In a pinch, navy beans will work fine.

# CHRISTMAS LIMA BEANS AND QUINOA
## WITH BEETS AND AVOCADO

*Serves 4 to 6*

**5 SMALL BEETS**

**EXTRA-VIRGIN OLIVE OIL** for drizzling

**½ CUP QUINOA**

**3 CUPS WELL-DRAINED, COOKED CHRISTMAS LIMA BEANS** (page 23), warmed slightly

**½ SMALL SWEET ONION**, thinly sliced

**1 AVOCADO**

### DRESSING

**2 TABLESPOONS FRESH LEMON JUICE**

**1 TABLESPOON CIDER VINEGAR**

**1 TEASPOON HONEY**

**⅓ CUP EXTRA-VIRGIN OLIVE OIL**

**SALT AND FRESHLY GROUND PEPPER**

*I loved the idea of using quinoa, an indigenous Incan super-grain loaded with protein, but it reminded me of a sad cousin to couscous. Sometimes it tasted bitter and it often seemed light and boring in comparison to rice. I experimented successfully with new recipes and now I eat quinoa at least weekly. Different brands of quinoa are cleaned in different ways so don't give up on quinoa. I promise you it will become one of your favorite grains. If your brand of quinoa is bitter, soak it for 4 to 6 hours, which removes some of the characteristic bitterness, improves the texture, and makes the quinoa more digestible.*

Preheat the oven to 400°F. Scrub the beets and dry them. Put in a medium bowl and drizzle with olive oil. Wrap the beets in 2 separate aluminum foil packages, putting like-sized beets with like-sized beets. Roast until tender, about 45 minutes. When the beets are cool enough to handle, slip off the skins with your fingers. Cut the beets into ¼-inch-thick wedges. Put in a large salad bowl.

Rinse the quinoa under cold running water. Bring a medium saucepan of generously salted water to a boil. Add the quinoa, reduce the heat to low, and simmer until the quinoa is fluffy but still slightly crunchy, 15 to 20 minutes. Drain and rinse quickly under cool running water. Drain well and add to the beets.

Add the beans and onion to the salad bowl. Cut the avocado in half lengthwise and remove the pit, leaving each half in the skin. Cut each half lengthwise into ¼-inch-thick slices. Then cut the slices crosswise into thirds. Using a spoon, scoop the avocado from the skin and add to the bowl. Toss gently.

**Make the dressing:** In a small bowl, whisk together the lemon juice, vinegar, and honey. Drizzle in the olive oil in a thin, steady stream, whisking continuously until the dressing comes together. Season to taste with salt and pepper.

Pour the dressing over the salad, toss, adjust the seasonings, and serve at room temperature within 2 hours.

# ABC
## BEAN SALAD

*Serves 8 to 10*

---

### DRESSING

¼ CUP RED WINE VINEGAR

1 GARLIC CLOVE, MINCED

⅔ CUP EXTRA-VIRGIN OLIVE OIL

---

1 POUND MIXED FIRM BEANS such as *borlotti*, flageolet, *mayacoba*, yellow Indian woman, Vallarta, Santa Maria *pinquito*, scarlet runner, and/or cannellini, cooked (page 23), warmed slightly, and drained well

2 SMALL YELLOW or RED BELL PEPPERS, seeded and diced

3 GREEN ONIONS, white and pale green parts, thinly sliced

½ CUP CHOPPED FRESH FLAT-LEAF PARSLEY

SALT AND FRESHLY GROUND PEPPER

*Once in a while I run across people I affectionately call "bean freaks." They are real fans of beans but have been ill served by commercial agriculture and tend to go a little nuts the first time they have access to all the great heirloom varieties grown by specialty producers. Alexis Handelman, of Alexis Baking Company, is a bean freak, and one of the highlights of my delivery route is watching Alexis and her talented head chef, Carmen, dig through the delivery box like two greedy kids on Christmas morning. Alexis and Carmen came up with this delicious salad. They don't have any hard-and-fast rules about bean varieties. If they find something interesting at the farmers' market, like asparagus, artichokes, or cherry tomatoes, it can end up in this salad.*

**Make the dressing:** In a small bowl, whisk together the red wine vinegar and garlic. Slowly drizzle in the olive oil, whisking continuously until the dressing comes together.

In a large salad bowl, combine the beans, bell peppers, onions, and parsley, and season generously with salt and pepper. Pour the dressing over the salad and toss. Serve at room temperature.

# BANANA AND FLOR DE JUNIO BEAN SALAD

*Serves 6 to 8*

1 MEDIUM CUCUMBER, peeled

1 LARGE TART APPLE

2 TO 3 SERRANO CHILES

1½ CUPS WELL-DRAINED, COOKED *FLOR DE JUNIO* BEANS (page 23), warmed slightly

1¾ TEASPOONS INDIAN BLACK SALT

1 HEAPING TEASPOON *CHANNA MASALA*

1 TEASPOON CUMIN SEEDS, toasted and ground (page 29)

⅓ TO ½ CUP TAMARIND CHUTNEY

¾ TO 1 CUP FRESH LEMON JUICE

6 RIPE BANANAS

½ CUP FRESH CILANTRO LEAVES

TABLE SALT

*Indian cooks often mix sweet, savory, spicy, and tart ingredients into salads and snacks. This Punjabi salad is the family recipe of a friend, Shelly Puri, and is unusual in that it uses New World beans. You might be a little skeptical about the combination here, but the salad is surprisingly delicious, is filled with lively flavors, and is definitely a new take on beans. This is the kind of salad that's great at room temperature and works with any kind of barbecue. The Indian spices are readily available in urban areas at Indian grocery stores or by mail order.*

Cut each cucumber in half lengthwise, seed, and then cut the lengths into quarters. Cut each quarter crosswise into ¼-inch slices. Leaving the apple unpeeled, cut it in half and then cut each half into ¼-inch-thick slices, removing the core. Cut the slices crosswise into ½-inch pieces. Cut the chiles crosswise into ¼-inch-thick slices, leaving the seeds intact.

In a large salad bowl, combine the cucumber, apple, and chiles. Add the beans, black salt, *channa masala*, cumin, chutney, and lemon juice. Toss to blend.

Peel and cut each banana in half lengthwise, and then cut each half crosswise into ¼-inch pieces. Add the bananas and cilantro to the salad and mix gently. Taste and adjust the seasonings with chutney, lemon juice, or table salt. Serve at room temperature within 2 hours.

**Substitution Note:** In India, this salad would more likely be made with chickpeas, but New World beans of the pinto variety are also used.

# NOPAL AND BEAN SALAD
## WITH CILANTRO

*Serves 4*

---

**2 NOPAL PADDLES**, prepared and cooked (page 29)

**1 CUP WELL-DRAINED, COOKED BLACK BEANS** (page 23), warmed slightly

**½ RED ONION**, chopped

**½ CUP CRUMBLED *QUESO FRESCO*, or ½ CUP CUBED MONTEREY JACK CHEESE** (¼-inch cubes)

**¼ CUP CHOPPED FRESH CILANTRO**

**1 CUP MIXED SALAD GREENS**

**SALT AND FRESHLY GROUND PEPPER**

### DRESSING

**2 GARLIC CLOVES**, minced

**2 TABLESPOONS FRESH LIME JUICE**

**2 TABLESPOONS SUNFLOWER** or **GRAPESEED OIL**

**2 TABLESPOONS EXTRA-VIRGIN OLIVE OIL**

*Right after beans, my passions lie with cactus plants. I love that I can do so little and get so much back. The plant produces a vegetable, the paddles (nopales), and a fruit, the prickly pears (tunas). If the plant is growing on a southern slope, and you give it a little water and the occasional trim, it will give back like no other. This salad incorporates all the ingredients and flavors I love, and it's easy to make ahead. Just add the dressing at the last minute.*

In a large salad bowl, combine the nopales, beans, onion, cheese, cilantro, and greens. Toss to combine.

**Make the dressing:** In a small bowl, whisk together the garlic and lime juice. Slowly drizzle in the sunflower and olive oils, whisking continually until the dressing comes together.

Pour the dressing over the salad. Toss well and season with salt and pepper.

*chapter*

# 4

# SIDE
## DISHES

# POT
## BEANS

*Serves 6 to 8*

1 TABLESPOON LARD (see below) or
EXTRA-VIRGIN OLIVE OIL

½ MEDIUM WHITE or RED ONION, chopped

2 GARLIC CLOVES, smashed

1 POUND BEANS OF YOUR CHOICE, soaked (page 21)

SALT

4 KEY LIMES, cut in half, for serving

FINELY CHOPPED WHITE or RED ONION, for serving

¼ CUP CHOPPED FRESH CILANTRO for serving

*Here's my confession. I love trying new things and getting excited about new ingredients and new ways to use them. And yet, the reality is this dish, pot beans, or frijoles de olla, is my favorite way to eat beans. It is a simply made recipe that cooks the beans slowly and adorns them with just a few additions. Any heirloom bean will taste wonderful this way, though this particular serving suggestion does bring to mind a pintolike bean. A bowl of beans, a salad, and either tortillas or bread, and I'm set.*

In a stockpot over medium heat, warm the lard. Add the onion and garlic and sauté until soft and fragrant, about 10 minutes. Add the beans and their soaking water. Add more cold water if needed to cover the beans by at least 1 inch. Raise the heat to high, bring to a rapid boil, and cook for 5 minutes. Reduce the heat so that the beans are barely simmering and cook, partially covered, until the beans are soft, about 1 to 1½ hours.

Season the beans judiciously with salt, keeping in mind that it takes time for the beans to absorb the salt.

Ladle the beans into warmed bowls. Diners top their servings with a squeeze of key lime, a spoonful of chopped onions, and a sprinkling of cilantro.

## *Rendering Lard*

Lard has a bad reputation but not a fair one. Lard is a monounsaturated fat high in oleic acid. On some level, fat is fat and too much of any fat is obviously not going to help you. If you're going to eat lard, make sure it's high quality. The bleached white lard sold in grocery stores in bricks or tubs is overprocessed and contains hydrogenated oils and chemicals, making it useless for our needs.

If you have a Mexican or ethnic butcher, there's a good chance they are selling their own lard. Or you can render it yourself. Saving bacon drippings is the easiest, but the smoky flavor can overwhelm many dishes. Rendering lard only requires you to chop up some pork fat (about 1 pound) and place it in a cast-iron skillet with about ½ cup of water (so the fat doesn't scorch) in a 375°F oven for about 45 minutes or until the fat has melted. Take the pan out of the oven and allow it to cool. Strain the lard into clean containers and use as needed. Save any little meaty bits you strained for the bean pot. One pound of back fat will yield about 1½ cups of lard. Use about ½ cup water per pound of fat.

# DRUNKEN
## BEANS

*Serves 4*

**4 CUPS COOKED PINTO, RIO ZAPE, RED APPALOOSA,** or
**ANASAZI BEANS** (page 23), in their broth

**1 BOTTLE LAGER BEER**

**2 SLICES HIGH-QUALITY BACON**, diced

**½ MEDIUM YELLOW** or **WHITE ONION**, chopped

**3 GARLIC CLOVES**, finely chopped

**3 TO 4 SERRANO CHILES**, seeded if desired and chopped

**½ POUND CREMINI MUSHROOMS**, sliced

**SALT AND FRESHLY GROUND PEPPER**

**CORN TORTILLAS**, warmed, for serving

**LIME WEDGES** for serving

*Just as baked beans are to an Easterner, a bowl of drunken beans,* borrachos, *is comfort food beyond compare to a Westerner like myself. These beans, a good salad, and a bottle of beer to wash it all down are about all you need. The measurements and directions are very forgiving, so don't be afraid to improvise and come up with your own tradition.*

In a stockpot over medium heat, warm the beans and their broth. Add the beer and simmer to cook off some of the beer, about 20 minutes.

Meanwhile, in a small, heavy skillet over medium heat, sauté the bacon until the fat is nearly rendered and the bacon is brown, about 10 minutes. Remove with a slotted spoon and drain on paper towels. Pour off all but 1 tablespoon of the fat in the pot. Add the onion, garlic, and chiles, and sauté over medium heat until soft and fragrant, about 10 minutes. Add the mushrooms and sauté until wilted and soft, about 10 minutes. Stir in the cooked bacon.

Add the mushroom mixture to the beans, season with salt and pepper, and cook until the flavors are blended, about 10 minutes.

Serve the beans with warm tortillas and lime wedges.

# REFRIED
## BEANS

*Serves 4*

1 TABLESPOON PLUS 1 TEASPOON LARD (page 110) or
EXTRA-VIRGIN OLIVE OIL

¼ MEDIUM WHITE ONION, thinly sliced

½ POUND RIO ZAPE, ANASAZI, *FLOR DE JUNIO*, or PINTO
BEANS, cooked (page 23), with reserved broth

SALT

*There are a few foods that I just can't stop eating, and properly made refried beans is one of them. The more I experiment, the more I discover that* refritos *belong with lots of different dishes. For instance, try a grilled cheese sandwich with a nice thin layer of* refritos *and maybe some pickled onions. If you decide to make the beans authentically with lard, be sure you use rendered lard (page 110), not the processed white bricks that pass for lard in supermarkets. I often use olive oil, with great success, but aficionados will tell you this isn't authentic.*

In a large, heavy skillet over medium heat, warm the lard. Add the onion and sauté, until soft and fragrant, about 10 minutes.

Add the beans along with about ½ cup of their broth. Cook the beans, mashing them with a potato masher to incorporate the soft onions. The longer you cook the beans, the smoother, richer, and better they will be, so plan on about 15 minutes of continuous cooking and mashing. When done, the beans will be smooth and thick with a bit of bean texture, the onions will have disappeared, and a spoon run through the beans will leave a trail. Season to taste with salt.

# CUBAN
# BLACK
# BEANS
## SOFRITO

*Serves 4 to 6*

---

**1 POUND BLACK VALENTINE BEANS**, soaked (page 21)

**2 TABLESPOONS SAFFLOWER** or **GRAPESEED OIL**

**1 SMALL WHITE ONION**, chopped

**2 GARLIC CLOVES**, finely chopped

**½ MEDIUM GREEN BELL PEPPER**, seeded and chopped

**1 JALAPEÑO CHILE**, chopped

**2 TABLESPOONS CIDER VINEGAR**

**¼ CUP FRESH CILANTRO LEAVES**

**¼ TEASPOON SPANISH SMOKED PAPRIKA**

**SALT AND FRESHLY GROUND PEPPER**

*The beans here are cooked first in water, then are flavored with a mixture of aromatic vegetables and seasonings, called* sofrito. Sofrito *can be made more like a fresh salsa, but in this dish it is sautéed until it develops an almost smoky flavor. Serve with the Cuban Roast Pork (page 143) or use as a base for Moors and Christians (page 114).*

Put the beans and their soaking water in a stockpot and add more cold water if needed to cover the beans by at least 1 inch. Bring to a rapid boil and cook for 5 minutes. Reduce the heat so that the beans are barely simmering and cook until the beans are nearly soft, about 1 hour.

Meanwhile, in a medium, heavy skillet over medium-high heat, warm the safflower oil. Add the onion, garlic, bell pepper, and chile and sauté until the vegetables are very aromatic and beginning to brown, 8 to 10 minutes. Add the vinegar, cilantro, paprika, and salt and pepper to taste and continue to cook, stirring, for 2 to 3 minutes.

Scoop 1 cup of the beans from the pot and add to the skillet. Using a potato masher, mash the beans with the *sofrito*. Add to the pot of simmering beans and season to taste with salt and pepper. Simmer until the beans are tender and flavorful, 30 to 40 minutes.

# MOORS
## AND
# CHRISTIANS

*Serves 4*

2 TABLESPOONS EXTRA-VIRGIN OLIVE OIL

½ MEDIUM YELLOW or WHITE ONION, chopped

2 GARLIC CLOVES, finely chopped

½ MEDIUM GREEN BELL PEPPER, seeded and chopped

1 JALAPEÑO CHILE, finely chopped

1 CUP LONG-GRAIN WHITE RICE

1 BAY LEAF

2 CUPS WATER

1 TEASPOON SALT

2 CUPS CUBAN BLACK BEANS *SOFRITO* (page 113), drained

FRESH CILANTRO LEAVES for garnishing

*In this dish, the black beans represent the Moors and the white rice the Christians, symbolizing the ethnic conflict in thirteenth-century Spain. It's all much simpler on your plate. The combination is a delicious Cuban classic that's easy to make and works as a side dish with pork. When preparing Cuban Black Beans Sofrito for this dish, you can leave all the beans whole rather than mash some of them.*

In a small Dutch oven or other heavy pot with a lid over medium-high heat, warm the olive oil. Add the onion, garlic, bell pepper, and chile. Sauté until the vegetables are soft, fragrant, and beginning to brown, about 10 minutes. Add the rice and stir to coat thoroughly with the oil. Add the bay leaf, water, salt, and beans. Reduce the heat to low, cover, and cook at a very slow simmer until the rice is tender and most of the liquid is absorbed, about 20 minutes. You may check the beans and rice toward the end of the cooking time to make sure the water level is not too low and add a bit more water if needed, but you should leave the beans and rice as undisturbed as possible.

Remove from the heat and let sit, covered, for 10 minutes before serving. Garnish each serving with cilantro.

# SCARLET RUNNER BEANS IN CHILE SAUCE

## WITH STUFFED SQUASH BLOSSOMS

*Serves 4 to 6*

**1 POUND SCARLET RUNNER** or **OTHER RUNNER BEANS**, soaked (page 21)

**4 ANCHO CHILES**, seeded

**HOT WATER**

**1 SMALL WHITE ONION**, quartered

**3 GARLIC CLOVES**

**ABOUT 1 CUP HOMEMADE** (see page 130) or **PURCHASED CHICKEN BROTH** or **WATER**

**1 TEASPOON CUMIN SEEDS**, toasted and ground (page 29)

**SALT AND FRESHLY GROUND PEPPER**

**3 OR 4 MIXED YELLOW AND GREEN SUMMER SQUASH**, cut into bite-size chunks

**CHOPPED FRESH CILANTRO** for garnishing

*Using runner beans and squash in a single dish is one of my favorite ways to cut down on meat consumption without compromising on a substantial meal. If you're not up to preparing stuffed squash blossoms, these chile-spiked beans and squash make a taco filling to remember.*

Begin cooking the beans as directed on page 23.

Meanwhile, put the chiles in a small bowl, add hot water to cover, and soak until soft, about 15 minutes. Drain the chiles and put them in a blender with the onion and garlic. Purée until smooth, adding some of the chicken broth or water to thin the mixture if necessary. The texture should be a bit thicker than heavy cream. You should have about 1½ cups chile purée. In a small, heavy skillet over medium-low heat, cook the purée, stirring and tasting occasionally, until the bitter flavor begins to mellow, about 15 minutes. Add the cumin and salt and pepper to taste and cook for 10 minutes to blend flavors.

When the beans are beginning to soften, after about 1 hour, add the chile purée and season to taste with salt and pepper.

Toss the squash in salt and let drain in a colander for 30 minutes. Rinse the squash and squeeze to remove the excess water. Add the squash to the beans and simmer until tender, about 15 minutes. When the beans are ready, keep them warm while you start cooking the squash blossoms.

*continued-*

# SCARLET RUNNER BEANS IN CHILE SAUCE
## WITH STUFFED SQUASH BLOSSOMS

*-continued*

### SQUASH BLOSSOMS

24 SQUASH BLOSSOMS

6 OUNCES *QUESO FRESCO*

2 EGGS

¼ CUP WATER

¾ CUP ALL-PURPOSE FLOUR

¼ CUP FINE YELLOW CORNMEAL

½ TEASPOON SALT

¼ TEASPOON FRESHLY GROUND PEPPER

SAFFLOWER OR GRAPESEED OIL for frying

**Prepare the blossoms:** Pinch off the stems. Carefully stuff each blossom with 1½ to 2 teaspoons of the *queso fresco*. Gently twist the ends to close. In a shallow bowl, beat together the eggs and water. In a shallow dish, mix together the flour, cornmeal, salt, and pepper. Dip each stuffed squash blossom in the beaten eggs and let the excess drip back into the bowl. Gently roll each blossom in the cornmeal mixture to coat completely. Refrigerate the blossoms for at least 15 minutes or up to 30 minutes.

Preheat the oven to 225°F. Line a baking sheet with paper towels.

Pour safflower oil to a depth of ½ to ¾ inch into a heavy 10- or 12-inch skillet. Set over medium-high heat and warm the oil until it is shimmering and a stuffed squash blossom dipped into the oil sizzles briskly without smoking. Fry the blossoms a few at a time, turning once with tongs, until golden brown, 1 to 2 minutes per side. Transfer to the prepared baking sheet and keep warm in the oven.

Serve the beans in warmed bowls garnished with chopped cilantro and accompanied by the fried squash blossoms.

# SCARLET RUNNER BEANS
## WITH PORCINI AND TRUMPET MUSHROOMS

*Serves 4*

½ OUNCE DRIED PORCINI MUSHROOMS

½ CUP HOT WATER

2 TABLESPOONS UNSALTED BUTTER

1 TABLESPOON EXTRA-VIRGIN OLIVE OIL, plus more for drizzling

5 GARLIC CLOVES, finely chopped

1 MEDIUM SHALLOT, cut in half and thinly sliced

¼ POUND ROYAL TRUMPET MUSHROOMS, thinly sliced

SALT

½ CUP DRY RED WINE

FRESHLY GROUND PEPPER

3 CUPS DRAINED, COOKED SCARLET RUNNER BEANS (page 23), with reserved broth

FRESHLY GRATED PARMESAN CHEESE for garnishing

*When people ask me about making scarlet runners, I normally say, "After you cook them, sauté them with wild mushrooms and slightly too much garlic." That's exactly what this dish does. If you cannot find trumpet mushrooms, use cremini.*

Put the porcini in a small bowl, add the hot water, and soak until soft, about 15 minutes.

In a large, heavy skillet over medium heat, melt the butter with the 1 tablespoon olive oil. Add the garlic and shallot and sauté until fragrant, 2 to 3 minutes. Add the trumpet mushrooms and a pinch of salt. Reduce the heat to low and cook, stirring and tossing occasionally, until the mushrooms begin to wilt, 3 to 4 minutes. If the pan becomes dry, add 1 or 2 tablespoons of the porcini soaking liquid.

Drain the porcini, reserving the soaking liquid. Chop the porcini, add to the pan, and cook until the mushrooms begin to brown, 3 to 4 minutes. Add 2 to 3 tablespoons of the porcini soaking liquid and the wine. Season to taste with salt and pepper, raise the heat to medium-high, and cook, stirring and scraping up any browned bits from the bottom of the pan. When the alcohol has dissipated, add the beans and simmer for 10 minutes to blend the flavors. Add the bean broth or porcini soaking liquid if a soupier dish is desired. Season to taste with salt and pepper. Garnish the beans with a drizzle of olive oil and a sprinkling of Parmesan cheese.

**Substitution Note:** White runner beans aren't quite right for this recipe, so try one of the large, creamy cranberry beans such as *borlotti*.

# INDIAN-SPICED
# CRANBERRY BEANS

*Serves 4*

½ **POUND CRANBERRY BEANS**, cooked (page 23), in their broth

2 **TABLESPOONS EXTRA-VIRGIN OLIVE OIL**

½ **MEDIUM YELLOW ONION**, sliced

4 **GARLIC CLOVES**, finely chopped

1½-**INCH PIECE FRESH GINGER**, peeled and finely chopped

2 **CARDAMOM PODS**, crushed

2 **TEASPOONS CUMIN SEEDS**, lightly crushed

1 **TEASPOON FENNEL SEEDS**, lightly crushed

1 **TEASPOON CORIANDER SEEDS**, lightly crushed

1 **SERRANO CHILE**, sliced

3 **FRESH** or **CANNED PLUM TOMATOES**, chopped and drained

**SALT AND FRESHLY GROUND PEPPER**

**CHOPPED FRESH CILANTRO** for garnishing

*Sheamus Feeley is the hot young chef who heads up the kitchen at the Rutherford Grill, a relaxed bistro packed with locals and tourists alike. The restaurant was one of the first to buy my beans when I was working the local farmers' markets. This spicy recipe was inspired by one Feeley made with garam masala as an experiment. It turns out that cranberry beans take to Indian spices quite well.*

In a soup pot over medium heat, gently warm the beans and their broth.

In a small, heavy skillet over medium heat, warm the oil. Add the onion, garlic, and ginger and sauté until soft and fragrant, about 10 minutes. Raise heat to medium-high, add the cardamom, cumin, fennel, coriander, chile, and tomatoes, and cook, stirring, for 2 to 3 minutes. Add the spice mixture to the beans, season to taste with salt and pepper, and continue to cook for about 10 minutes to blend the flavors. Serve the beans garnished with chopped cilantro.

**Substitution Note:** Good Mother Stallard or Santa Maria *pinquito* beans would work nicely.

# JACOB'S
# CATTLE
# BEANS
## WITH PANCETTA
## AND SAGE

*Serves 4*

½ **POUND JACOB'S CATTLE BEANS**, soaked (page 21)

3 **TABLESPOONS EXTRA-VIRGIN OLIVE OIL**, plus more for drizzling

½ **MEDIUM YELLOW ONION**, chopped

1 **MEDIUM CARROT**, peeled and chopped

2 **CELERY STALKS**, chopped

3 **GARLIC CLOVES**, finely chopped

¼ **POUND PANCETTA**, diced

2 **TABLESPOONS CHOPPED FRESH SAGE**

**SALT AND FRESHLY GROUND PEPPER**

**FRESHLY GRATED PARMESAN CHEESE** for garnishing

*Jacob's cattle is one of the few heirloom varieties that many people know, but these beans tend to go straight to baked beans. I find the texture similar to that of new potatoes. On their own, they are good enough to use in a simple dish like this. In fact, it would be easy to make this every night.*

Put the beans and their soaking water in a soup pot and add more cold water if needed to cover the beans by 1 inch. Bring to a boil, reduce the heat to low, and simmer, partially covered, until beans just begin to soften, about 30 minutes.

In a medium, heavy skillet over medium-low heat, warm the 3 tablespoons olive oil. Add the onion, carrot, celery, garlic, pancetta, 1 tablespoon of the sage, and a little salt and pepper, and sauté very slowly to draw out the flavor of the aromatics and pancetta, about 20 minutes. Do not allow the vegetables and pancetta to brown.

Add the vegetables and pancetta to the beans, season with salt, and simmer, partially covered, until the beans are tender, about 1 hour. Check the water level often and add more water if needed. This dish is best when the beans are a little soupy. During the final 5 minutes of cooking, add the remaining 1 tablespoon sage and adjust the seasonings.

Serve the beans in warmed shallow bowls. Drizzle with olive oil and sprinkle with Parmesan cheese.

**Substitution Note:** Cranberry beans will also work nicely in this simple recipe, or try Good Mother Stallard beans.

# CANNELLINI
## WITH
# TOMATOES AND SAGE

*Serves 6*

### OVEN-CURED TOMATOES

**6 PLUM TOMATOES**

**1 TABLESPOON CHOPPED FRESH FLAT-LEAF PARSLEY**

**3 TO 4 TABLESPOONS EXTRA-VIRGIN OLIVE OIL**

**SALT**

*In Florence, small game birds, uccelletti, are prepared with tomato and sage. For this recipe, fagioli all'uccelletto, the beans are similarly cooked. This version comes from Marco Canora and Edward Higgins, chefs at New York's red-hot Insieme Restaurant. Traditionally, Marco's family in Tuscany would soak the beans for two whole days. The tomatoes need to be prepared a day in advance.*

**Make the tomatoes:** Preheat the oven to 200°F. Core the tomatoes. Slice each tomato nearly in half lengthwise, taking care not to cut all the way through so the halves remain attached. In a medium bowl, combine the tomatoes, parsley, extra-virgin olive oil, and salt to taste. Toss to coat. Arrange the tomatoes, cut side down, in a single layer on a rack set over a baking sheet. Bake until the liquid is evaporated and the tomatoes are shriveled and reduced in size, but not completely dry, about 10 hours. Chop the tomatoes and set aside.

**1 POUND RUNNER CANNELLINI** or *CELLINI* **BEANS**, soaked
(page 21)

**1 MEDIUM CARROT**, peeled and quartered

**1 CELERY STALK**, cut into thirds

**1 GARLIC HEAD**, halved

**3 FRESH SAGE SPRIGS**

**3 FRESH ROSEMARY SPRIGS**

**SALT**

**¼ CUP SAFFLOWER** or **GRAPESEED OIL** for frying

**20 FRESH SAGE LEAVES**

**½ CUP EXTRA-VIRGIN OLIVE OIL**, plus oil for drizzling

**2 GARLIC CLOVES**, thinly sliced

**3 TABLESPOONS CHOPPED FRESH SAGE**

**FRESHLY GROUND PEPPER**

In a stockpot, combine the beans and their soaking water, carrot, celery, and garlic head. Put the sage sprigs and rosemary sprigs on a piece of cheesecloth, gather the corners, and tie the bundle securely. Add to the pot. Add more cold water if needed to cover the beans by at least 1 inch. Bring to a simmer over medium-high heat and cook, partially covered, until the beans are nearly soft, about 1 hour. Season with salt and continue cooking the beans until tender, about 30 minutes. Allow the beans to cool in their broth. Remove and discard the vegetables, garlic head, and cheesecloth bundle. Drain the beans, reserving the broth.

In a small, heavy skillet over medium-high heat, warm the safflower oil until it is shimmering. Add the sage leaves, 4 at a time, and fry until they are crisp but remain bright green, 10 to 15 seconds. Remove with tongs to a paper towel to drain.

In a large, heavy skillet over medium-low heat, warm the ½ cup olive oil. Add the sliced garlic and chopped sage, and sauté until aromatic. Add the chopped tomatoes and cook just until they begin to break down, 3 to 5 minutes.

Add the cooked beans to the skillet along with 1 cup of the reserved broth. Continue cooking until the liquid has reduced and leaves a glossy shine on the beans. Season to taste with salt and pepper and drizzle generously with olive oil.

Transfer the beans to a serving dish and top with the fried sage leaves.

# BAKED BEANS
## NEW ENGLAND STYLE

*Serves 6 to 8*

1 POUND EUROPEAN SOLDIER, WHITE NAVY, or YELLOW EYE BEANS, soaked (page 21)

2 TEASPOONS DRY MUSTARD

1 TABLESPOON TOMATO PASTE

1 TEASPOON SALT

⅓ CUP DARK MOLASSES

¼ CUP LIGHTLY PACKED BROWN SUGAR

2 TABLESPOONS MAPLE SYRUP

½ POUND SALT PORK, rinsed, dried, and scored in several places with a sharp knife (optional)

½ LARGE YELLOW ONION, thinly sliced

SALT AND FRESHLY GROUND PEPPER

*This potluck classic is easy to put together and requires almost no attention while it cooks. Leave the salt pork out for a vegetarian version that's nearly as good. You won't need to change anything. Just add more salt. The beans can also be served as a main dish, accompanied with a green salad.*

Put the beans and their soaking water in a stockpot and add more cold water if needed to cover the beans by 1 inch. Bring to a boil. Reduce the heat to low and simmer, uncovered, until the beans are beginning to soften, about 1 hour.

Preheat the oven to 250°F.

Drain the beans, reserving the broth. If necessary add enough water to the broth to measure 2 cups. In a medium bowl, whisk together the broth, mustard, tomato paste, salt, molasses, brown sugar, and maple syrup.

Put half of the beans in a large Dutch oven or other heavy pot with a lid. Top with the salt pork (if using) and half of the sliced onion. Add the remaining beans and top with the remaining onion. Pour the broth mixture over the beans, cover, and bake until the beans are soft, the pork is meltingly tender, and the sauce is thick and clings to the beans, 5 to 7 hours. Stop and check occasionally to make sure there is enough liquid in the beans, and add water if necessary, but not too much. Season to taste with salt and pepper.

# RED BEANS AND RICE

*Serves 6*

3 TABLESPOONS EXTRA-VIRGIN OLIVE OIL

1 MEDIUM YELLOW ONION, chopped

2 CELERY STALKS, chopped

½ MEDIUM GREEN BELL PEPPER, seeded and chopped

2 GARLIC CLOVES, finely chopped

1 POUND RED NIGHTFALL BEANS, soaked (page 21)

ONE 1-POUND HAM SHANK

1 BAY LEAF

½ TEASPOON DRIED THYME

½ TEASPOON DRIED OREGANO

½ TEASPOON CAYENNE PEPPER

SALT AND FRESHLY GROUND PEPPER

COOKED LONG-GRAIN WHITE RICE for serving

BOTTLED HOT SAUCE or PICKLED JALAPEÑOS for serving

*Red beans and rice were traditionally made on Monday wash days because the dish doesn't need tending. Southern cooks often use kidney beans but red nightfall beans are even better. This rich dish benefits from a sprinkle of vinegar, which is why, in the South, table condiments often include a dish with pickled jalapeños in vinegar. Most people just spoon a little of the vinegar into the beans. I've also seen the dish eaten with sauerkraut—not a traditional garnish, but it makes sense when you recall that beans and pork are traditional sauerkraut companions.*

In a large Dutch oven or other heavy pot with a lid over medium-high heat, warm the olive oil. Add the onion, celery, bell pepper, and garlic and sauté until soft and fragrant, about 10 minutes. Add the beans and their soaking water and then the ham shank. Add enough cold water to cover the beans by 1 inch. Add the bay leaf, thyme, oregano, and cayenne. Bring to a boil, reduce the heat to low, and simmer, partially covered, until the beans begin to break down and the ham starts to fall off the bone, 2 to 3 hours. Add water as needed to keep the ingredients submerged. Season to taste with salt and pepper.

Remove the ham from the pot and set aside to cool. Raise the heat to medium-high and cook the beans, uncovered, until thick and creamy, about 20 minutes. To help thicken them, you can use a wooden spoon to mash them against the sides of the pot or use an immersion blender to purée partially.

Remove the ham from the bone and shred. Return it to the pot. Cook until heated through. Taste and adjust the seasonings.

Serve the beans over cooked white rice. Pass the hot sauce at the table.

# FLORIDA BUTTER BEANS
## WITH CARAMELIZED ONIONS AND BACON

*Serves 4*

½ **POUND FLORIDA BUTTER BEANS**, soaked (page 21)

4 **SLICES HIGH-QUALITY BACON**, diced

2½ **MEDIUM YELLOW ONIONS**

2 **CELERY STALKS**, diced

2 **GARLIC CLOVES**, finely chopped

**SALT**

¾ **TEASPOON CHOPPED FRESH THYME LEAVES**

**FRESHLY GROUND PEPPER**

*Florida butter beans, sometimes known as calico pole beans, are baby lima beans. I grew up hating all lima beans because my mother, like many mothers in the 1960s, didn't quite know how to cook them to perfection. If you felt the same way, I urge you to give the heirloom varieties like this one another try.*

Put the beans and their soaking water in a stockpot and add more cold water if needed to cover the beans by 1 inch. Bring to a boil. Reduce the heat to low and simmer, partially covered, until the beans are beginning to soften, about 1 hour.

In a medium, heavy skillet over medium heat, sauté the bacon until the fat is rendered and the bacon is beginning to brown, 8 to 10 minutes. Remove with a slotted spoon and drain on paper towels.

Pour off all but 2 tablespoons of the bacon fat from the pan and reserve. Chop half of an onion and add to the pan over medium heat. Add the celery and garlic and sauté until the vegetables are soft and fragrant, about 10 minutes. Add to the beans, reduce the heat to low, cover, and simmer until the beans are tender, 1 to 1½ hours. When the beans are nearly soft, season them with salt.

Meanwhile, cut the remaining 2 whole onions in half, then cut into thin slices. Wipe out the skillet with a paper towel, pour in 2 tablespoons of the reserved bacon fat, and set over medium-low heat. Add the sliced onions and a few pinches of salt. Cook, stirring, until the onions wilt. Reduce the heat to low and cook, stirring occasionally, until the onions are medium brown, soft, and caramelized, 45 minutes to 1 hour. Add 2 tablespoons water and stir to loosen any browned bits on the bottom of the pan. Add the thyme and season to taste with salt and pepper. Add the bacon to the caramelized onions and heat gently.

Top each serving of beans with some of the caramelized onion–bacon mixture.

**Substitution Note:** Use Christmas lima beans.

# FLORIDA BUTTER BEAN SUCCOTASH
## WITH MINT AND GOAT CHEESE

*Serves 4*

**2 TABLESPOONS UNSALTED BUTTER**

**3 GREEN ONIONS**, white and pale green parts and some of the dark green tops, thinly sliced

**1½ CUPS FRESH CORN KERNELS** (2 medium ears)

**½ POUND FLORIDA BUTTER BEANS**, cooked (page 23) and drained

**SALT AND FRESHLY GROUND PEPPER**

**½ CUP HALVED CHERRY TOMATOES**

**2 TABLESPOONS CHOPPED FRESH MINT**

**¼ POUND FRESH GOAT CHEESE**

*Succotash is traditionally made with fresh limas, corn, and cream. This modern version takes some liberties by using dried heirlooms, but I think you'll agree they are worth it. Serve as a summer side dish with something from the grill or make it a complete meal with rice and a salad on a hot summer's evening.*

In a large saucepan over medium heat, melt the butter. Add the green onions and sauté for 2 to 3 minutes. Add the corn and sauté for 2 to 3 minutes. Add the beans and season to taste with salt and pepper. Remove from the heat, and toss in the tomatoes and mint.

Serve immediately, crumbling a little goat cheese over each portion.

**Substitution Note:** Try this recipe with Christmas lima beans or with fresh lima beans if you have them.

# 5

*chapter*

# MAIN DISHES
## AND CASSEROLES

# ENFRIJOLADAS WITH
# CHICKEN

*Serves 6*

---

**2 TABLESPOONS PLUS ⅓ CUP SAFFLOWER** or **GRAPESEED OIL**

**1 MEDIUM WHITE ONION**, chopped

**3 GARLIC CLOVES**, finely chopped

**½ POUND RIO ZAPE BEANS**, cooked (page 23) and drained

**ABOUT 2 CUPS HOMEMADE** (see page 130) or **PURCHASED CHICKEN BROTH**

**SALT**

**12 CORN TORTILLAS**

---

## FOR SERVING

**¼ CUP DICED WHITE ONION**

**2 CUPS SHREDDED CHICKEN** (page 130)

**ABOUT ⅓ CUP CRUMBLED *QUESO FRESCO***

**1½ AVOCADOS**, pitted, peeled, and cut into ¼-inch-thick slices

**⅓ CUP FRESH CILANTRO LEAVES**

*As a self-described bean freak, I think I hit a high C when I discovered* enfrijoladas. *Whereas enchiladas are tortillas dipped in a chili sauce,* enfrijoladas *are dipped in a bean sauce. Variations can be found all over Mexico but the most popular version seems to be the Oaxacan with black beans and a simple garnish of cilantro or* epazote, *along with finely diced raw onion.* Epazote *is a strong, leafy herb that is commonly paired with black beans and is said to aid digestion. While my choice is Rio Zape beans, you could use almost any pintolike bean such as eye of the goat or* flor de junio. *The addition of chicken, though not traditional, makes for a substantial meal.*

In a medium, heavy skillet over medium heat, warm the 2 tablespoons safflower oil. Add the onion and garlic and sauté until soft and fragrant, about 10 minutes. Let cool slightly and put in a food processor. Add the beans. Purée until smooth, adding the chicken broth until the beans are the consistency of thin porridge. Transfer to a skillet large enough to accommodate a tortilla. Set over low heat and warm the beans, stirring occasionally. Season to taste with salt and add more chicken broth if the beans seem thick.

Wipe out the skillet used for the onions and garlic and pour in the ⅓ cup oil. Heat over medium-high heat until the oil is shimmering but not smoking and a tortilla dipped in the oil sizzles gently. If it sizzles violently, turn down the heat a bit before testing again. If the tortilla doesn't sizzle at all, the oil will soak in too fast, making the tortillas greasy. Fry the tortillas one at a time, turning once, until softened but not turning brown and crisp, 3 or 4 seconds per side. Drain on paper towels.

Dip each tortilla in the warm puréed beans. The beans should cling but not too thickly. Add more broth if the beans need thinning. Fold the tortilla into quarters and place on a warmed serving dish in a single layer. Sprinkle with the onion, followed by the chicken, *queso fresco*, avocados, and cilantro. Alternatively, plate the servings, giving each person 2 *enfrijoladas*.

# *all-purpose*
# POACHED CHICKEN
## MEXICAN STYLE

**ONE 3- TO 4-POUND FREE-RANGE CHICKEN**

**½ MEDIUM YELLOW ONION**, thinly sliced

**5 GARLIC CLOVES**, crushed

**PINCH OF CUMIN SEEDS**

**½ TEASPOON DRIED MEXICAN OREGANO**

**2 PINCHES OF DRIED THYME**

**1 BAY LEAF**

**1 TEASPOON SALT**

**6 TO 10 PEPPERCORNS**

**3 OR 4 FRESH CILANTRO SPRIGS**

*When in doubt, poach a chicken. That's been my rule for some time now. With minimal fuss, you get enough cooked chicken for several meals and nearly a gallon of delicious chicken broth. You can even remove the skin before poaching and make cracklings. Lay the skin on a baking sheet and bake in a 200°F oven for 2 to 4 hours. Crumble the skin and add to salads as you would bacon, or use it to garnish beans. The rendered fat can be saved for browning the poached chicken meat. What an incredible value! Nothing is wasted. This recipe calls for a whole chicken, but a cut-up chicken will work as well. Keep in mind that the bones and dark meat add flavor and body, so don't skimp on them. Simmering the chicken and then letting it cool in its broth produces tender, juicy meat and a light yet flavorful broth.*

Remove the neck and giblets from the cavity. Rinse the chicken well. Place the chicken in a large stockpot, Add the heart, kidneys, and neck to the pot (save the liver for another use). Add the onion, garlic, cumin, oregano, thyme, bay leaf, salt, peppercorns, and cilantro sprigs. Pour in cold water to cover. Bring to a boil over medium-high heat, then immediately reduce the heat to the gentlest of simmers. Simmer for 20 minutes. Turn off the heat, cover the pot, and let the chicken stand undisturbed for 1 hour.

Remove the chicken from the broth and let cool for 20 minutes before refrigerating or shredding. Strain the broth into a shallow bowl and let cool for 20 minutes. Refrigerate for several hours or overnight to let the fat settle on top. Skim off the fat and transfer the broth to containers for storage. The broth can be refrigerated for up to 3 days and frozen for up to 3 months.

# PICADILLO AND CORN ENCHILADAS WITH
# SPICY RIO ZAPE BEAN SAUCE

*Serves 5 to 6*

## BEAN SAUCE

**4 DRIED NEW MEXICO CHILES**

**BOILING WATER**

**1 TEASPOON DRIED MEXICAN OREGANO**

**2 TABLESPOONS VEGETABLE OIL** such as sunflower or safflower

**1 MEDIUM WHITE ONION**, chopped

**3 GARLIC CLOVES**, finely chopped

**1 TEASPOON CUMIN SEEDS**, toasted and ground (page 29)

**4 CUPS RIO ZAPE BEANS**, cooked (page 23) and cooled in their broth

**SALT AND FRESHLY GROUND PEPPER**

*Picadillo is often translated as "hash," but that's a pretty deficient interpretation for such a complex tasting, easy-to-make standard that has its roots in the Middle East. The slow-cooked medley of beef, tomatoes, and olives is sometimes enjoyed as a main dish on its own or as a filling, mostly in chiles. Though this recipe seems complicated, the end result is well worth the many steps.*

**Make the bean sauce:** Slit the chiles and remove the seeds and stems. In a small, heavy skillet over medium-high heat, toast the chiles until they puff slightly and begin to emit a spicy fragrance, about 15 seconds per side. Watch them carefully so they don't burn. Place in a small bowl, add boiling water to cover, and let soak for 20 to 30 minutes. Let the pan cool and then in the same pan over medium heat, toast the oregano until fragrant, about 30 seconds. Transfer to a small bowl.

In a large, heavy skillet over medium heat, warm the vegetable oil. Add the onion and garlic and sauté until soft and fragrant, about 10 minutes. Add the cumin, oregano, and beans and cook for 10 to 15 minutes. Season to taste with salt. Let the beans cool briefly, then drain, reserving the broth. If necessary, add enough water to make 2 cups of broth. Drain the chiles, reserving the soaking water. Put the beans, 1 1/2 cups of the bean broth, and the chiles in a blender and purée until the mixture is the consistency of thick tomato sauce, adding more of the bean broth or chile soaking water if needed. Season to taste with salt and pepper and set aside.

*continued-*

# PICADILLO AND CORN ENCHILADAS WITH SPICY RIO ZAPE BEAN SAUCE

-continued

## FILLING

**3 TABLESPOONS VEGETABLE OIL** such as sunflower or safflower

**1 MEDIUM WHITE ONION,** chopped

**2 GARLIC CLOVES,** finely chopped

**1½ POUNDS LEAN GROUND BEEF**

**SALT**

**ONE 14.5-OUNCE CAN CHOPPED TOMATOES,** drained

**1 CUP PIMIENTO-STUFFED GREEN OLIVES,** roughly chopped

**½ CUP RAISINS**

**1 CUP FRESH** or **FROZEN CORN KERNELS**

**2 TABLESPOONS APPLE CIDER VINEGAR**

**FRESHLY GROUND PEPPER**

**⅓ CUP SAFFLOWER** or **GRAPESEED OIL**

**15 CORN TORTILLAS**

**½ CUP FINELY CHOPPED WHITE ONION** for garnishing

**½ CUP FRESH CILANTRO LEAVES** for garnishing

**Make the filling:** In a large, heavy skillet over medium heat, warm the vegetable oil. Add the onion and garlic and sauté until soft and fragrant, about 10 minutes. Add the beef, season lightly with salt, and cook just until it is no longer pink, breaking it up with a large spoon as it browns. Add the tomatoes, olives, and raisins and cook, stirring occasionally, for about 15 minutes. Add the corn and cider vinegar and season to taste with salt and pepper. Remove from heat.

Preheat the oven to 350°F. Spread a thin layer of bean sauce on the bottom of a 9-by-13-inch baking dish.

Pour the ⅓ cup safflower oil into a medium, heavy skillet and heat over medium-high heat until the oil is shimmering but not smoking and a tortilla dipped in the oil sizzles gently. If it sizzles violently, turn down the heat a bit before testing again. If the tortilla doesn't sizzle at all, the oil will soak in too fast, making the tortillas greasy. Fry the tortillas one at a time, turning once, until softened but not turning brown and crisp, 3 or 4 seconds per side. Drain on paper towels.

Put 3 to 4 tablespoons of the filling on each softened tortilla. Roll and place in a single layer, seam side down, in the baking dish. Top with the remaining sauce, spreading it evenly with a rubber spatula to make sure all the exposed tortilla surfaces are covered. Cover the dish with aluminum foil and bake until the sauce is hot and bubbly, about 15 minutes. Garnish each serving with onion and cilantro.

**Substitution Note:** The flavor of Rio Zapes is incomparable, but the dish will still be great with any pintolike bean, including Anasazi or *flor de junio* beans.

# MEXICAN TORTA MILANESA
## DE POLLO

*Serves 4*

2 BONELESS, SKINLESS CHICKEN BREAST HALVES

⅓ CUP ALL-PURPOSE FLOUR

1¼ TEASPOONS SALT

1⅓ CUPS PLAIN DRY BREAD CRUMBS

½ TEASPOON FRESHLY GROUND PEPPER

2 EGGS, beaten

⅓ CUP SAFFLOWER or GRAPESEED OIL

1 CUP REFRIED BEANS (page 112)

4 MEXICAN SANDWICH ROLLS, split lengthwise

2 TABLESPOONS UNSALTED BUTTER, at room temperature

ABOUT ¼ POUND *QUESO FRESCO*, crumbled

1 AVOCADO, pitted, peeled, and sliced

ABOUT ⅓ CUP SLICED PICKLED JALAPEÑO CHILES (page 140)

4 TABLESPOONS MEXICAN *CREMA* or SOUR CREAM

*This popular sandwich from Guadalajara is now a favorite wherever ex-pats from the state of Jalisco gather. It's a moist, indulgent mess of a sandwich that's often wrapped in paper, making it an ideal "to go" food. You can easily skip the chicken and make it a* torta de frijoles. *You'll find Mexican sandwich rolls, called* bolillos *or* teleras, *at Latin markets. If they are unavailable, use Italian white sandwich rolls.*

Place each chicken breast half between 2 sheets of plastic wrap. Pound with a meat mallet to ¼ inch thick.

On a small plate, combine the flour with ¼ teaspoon of the salt. On another small plate, combine the bread crumbs, remaining 1 teaspoon salt, and the pepper. Put the beaten eggs in a shallow bowl.

Coat each chicken breast half with flour, shaking off the excess. Dip in the beaten eggs, and then in bread crumbs, pressing the crumbs into the sticky egg to adhere them. Put the coated breasts on a plate.

In a large, heavy skillet over medium-high heat, warm the safflower oil. When the oil is very hot but not smoking, fry the coated breasts until golden brown and cooked through, 2 to 3 minutes per side. Remove to a paper towel–lined plate and cover to keep warm.

In a small, heavy skillet over low heat, warm the Refried Beans.

*continued–*

# MEXICAN TORTA MILANESA
## DE POLLO

*-continued*

Preheat the broiler. With your fingers, remove some of the crumb from the insides of each roll to make a shell for hold-ing the sandwich ingredients. Spread the cut sides of each roll with butter. Place the rolls, buttered side up, on a baking sheet and toast under the broiler until browned.

Cut each chicken breast in half. Spread the bottom of each roll with about 3 tablespoons of the beans. Top with about 1 tablespoon of the crumbled cheese and then with a piece of chicken. Lay one-fourth of the avocado slices evenly over the chicken. Top with 3 or 4 slices of pickled jalapeños. Spread 1 tablespoon of the *crema* on the cut side of the top of the roll. Set it on the sandwich and press down gently. Serve immediately.

# HUEVOS
## RANCHO GORDO

*Serves 2*

½ CUP DRAINED, COOKED ANASAZI, *FLOR DE JUNIO*,
RIO ZAPE, or BLACK BEANS (page 23), heated, with
1½ cups reserved broth

4 EGGS, at room temperature

4 CORN TORTILLAS

1 CUP CLASSIC RED SALSA (page 57)

½ CUP CRUMBLED *QUESO FRESCO* or GRATED
MONTEREY JACK

SALT

CHOPPED FRESH CILANTRO for garnishing

*At its most basic,* huevos rancheros *is a dish of eggs smoth-ered in salsa, refried beans, and tortillas. It's a great breakfast and healthy, too, but sometimes I'm feeling a little creative in the morning. Somewhere between the classic dish and eggs Benedict lies Huevos Rancho Gordo.*

In a medium saucepan or deep skillet over medium-low heat, warm the bean broth so it barely simmers. Add a little water if it seems thick. Break each egg into a cup, then gently slide the egg into the simmering liquid. Cook 2 eggs at a time. Poach the eggs, spooning the hot broth over them, until the whites are opaque and the yolks remain soft. Using a slotted spoon, remove to a plate and set aside.

Warm a large, heavy skillet or *comal* over medium-high heat. Heat each tortilla, turning, until soft and warm.

Place 1 tortilla on each plate. Top with 2 cooked eggs and about ¼ cup beans. Spoon on ½ cup of the salsa and sprinkle with ¼ cup of the cheese. Season with salt to taste and garnish with cilantro. Fold one of the remaining tortillas in quarters and tuck underneath the tortilla on the plate for use as a scoop. Repeat for the second plate.

# CHILES RELLENOS

## RANCHO GORDO

*Serves 2*

1 MEDIUM WHITE ONION, finely chopped

1 POUND MEXICAN CHORIZO, casings removed and meat crumbled

1 TO 2 TABLESPOONS SAFFLOWER or SUNFLOWER OIL (optional)

1 CUP COOKED WILD RICE

¼ CUP CHOPPED FRESH CILANTRO

4 POBLANO CHILES, roasted (page 29)

1 CUP REFRIED BEANS (page 112)

1 CUP GRATED *MANCHEGO* CHEESE

1 CUP CLASSIC RED SALSA (page 57)

*I grew up eating battered and fried chiles rellenos, stuffed mostly with gooey cheese. I still love them, but when I found a rare copy of the out-of-print* Los Chiles Rellenos en Mexico *by Mexico City's brilliant Ricardo Muñoz Zurita, I was inspired to think beyond deep-frying and experiment with poblano chiles. Poblanos have a thick, meaty quality and a denser flavor than bell peppers. Occasionally you get one with some heat, but normally they are mild.*

Preheat the oven to 350°F.

In a medium, heavy skillet over medium heat, sauté the onion and chorizo until the onion is soft and the chorizo is cooked through, about 10 minutes. The chorizo has enough fat, but if the mixture seems dry, add a little oil. Add the wild rice, gently toss, and cook just until heated through. Remove from heat and stir in the cilantro.

Cut a slit down the length of each chile and remove the seeds. Carefully fill each chile with ¼ cup of the Refried Beans, followed by one-fourth of the chorizo mixture. Place the chiles on a baking sheet, open side up, and sprinkle ¼ cup of the cheese over the opening of each chile.

Bake until the cheese is melted, about 10 minutes. Spoon ½ cup salsa on each plate and top with 2 chiles rellenos.

# CHILES RELLENOS

## WITH SUMMER VEGETABLES

*Serves 2*

3 TABLESPOONS EXTRA-VIRGIN OLIVE OIL

1 MEDIUM WHITE ONION, chopped

1 TEASPOON DRIED MEXICAN OREGANO

2 SMALL ZUCCHINI, cut into ¼-inch dice

1 CUP FRESH or FROZEN CORN KERNELS

1 CUP DRAINED, COOKED RED APPALOOSA BEANS (page 23)

4 POBLANO CHILES, roasted (page 29)

1 CUP GRATED *MANCHEGO* CHEESE

*If corn is in season, use fresh kernels. Otherwise, frozen is fine for this mix of summer vegetables.*

Preheat oven to 350°F.

In a medium, heavy skillet over medium heat, warm the olive oil. Sauté the onion and oregano until the onion is soft and fragrant, about 10 minutes. Add the zucchini and corn and cook until the zucchini is tender, 6 to 7 minutes. Add the beans, gently toss, and continue cooking just until heated through. Remove from the heat.

Cut a slit down the length of each chile and remove the seeds. Carefully fill each chile with one-fourth of the bean mixture. Place the chiles on a baking sheet, open side up, and sprinkle ¼ cup of the cheese over the opening of each chile. Bake until the cheese is melted, about 10 minutes.

**Substitution Note:** Any pintolike bean is perfect here.

# BEAN CHILA-QUILES

## WITH AVOCADO AND QUESO FRESCO

*Serves 2*

⅓ CUP SAFFLOWER or GRAPESEED OIL

6 CORN TORTILLAS, each cut into 8 triangles

1 CUP THREE-CHILE SALSA (page 56) or your favorite salsa

½ TO ¾ CUP DRAINED, COOKED EYE OF THE GOAT, ANASAZI, or RIO ZAPE BEANS (page 23), with about ½ cup reserved broth

3 EGGS, beaten

### FOR SERVING

CHOPPED FRESH CILANTRO

AVOCADO SLICES

*QUESO FRESCO*, crumbled

MEXICAN *CREMA* or SOUR CREAM

*There are as many* chilaquile *recipes as there are cooks. Traditions vary from region to region, but at its essence, the dish consists of fried tortilla pieces soaked in a chile sauce. Sometimes it's fresh salsa and sometimes a sauce made with dried chiles. Clever cooks add leftover poached chicken, carnitas (fried pork), and vegetables. Beans aren't traditional, but they're not unheard of in* chilaquiles *either. With this recipe and a few leftovers, you can have breakfast on the table in the time it takes to brew coffee.*

In a large, heavy skillet over medium-high heat, warm the safflower oil until it is shimmering but not smoking and a tortilla triangle placed in the oil sizzles on contact. Fry the tortilla triangles, stirring constantly, until brown and crisp, 3 to 4 minutes.

Carefully pour in the salsa (as it will bubble and splatter), and cook, stirring, until the tortillas soak up most of the salsa, about 1 minute. Add the beans and stir to heat through.

Using a wooden spoon, move the tortilla mixture to one side of the pan. Reduce the heat to low, pour the eggs into the empty side of the pan, and cook, stirring, until they are halfway set, about 2 minutes. Stir the eggs into the tortilla mixture and cook until the eggs are just set.

Divide the *chilaquiles* between 2 plates and pass the cilantro, avocado, *queso fresco*, and *crema* at the table.

# "taco truck"
# PICKLED JALAPEÑOS
## AND CARROTS

10 JALAPEÑO CHILES

¼ CUP SAFFLOWER or GRAPESEED OIL

2 MEDIUM CARROTS, peeled and cut on the diagonal into ¼-inch-thick slices

¼ CUP THINLY SLICED WHITE ONION

2 GARLIC CLOVES, smashed with the side of a knife

¾ CUP WHITE VINEGAR

1 BAY LEAF

1 TEASPOON DRIED MEXICAN OREGANO

5 PEPPERCORNS

1 TEASPOON COARSE SALT

2 TEASPOONS SUGAR

*These are really the ubiquitous chiles in escabèche so often served as an accompaniment to many dishes in restaurants and at taco trucks. Many places use canned pickled jalapeños, but the Dos Hermaños Taco Truck in Vallejo, California, has a particularly good homemade version. Dos Hermaños is noteworthy for two other reasons: it puts beans in its tacos (an unusual and welcome addition!), and it is almost smack dab in the middle between my home in Napa and my co-author Vanessa Barrington's in San Francisco, so it became a favorite stop while working on this book.*

Cut a slit down the length of each chile, leaving the stem intact. In a medium, heavy skillet over high heat, warm the safflower oil. Add the chiles and stir-fry until the skins are evenly blistered all over and they turn from bright green to dull green, about 8 minutes. Add the carrots, onion, and garlic and stir-fry for 2 minutes. Remove from the heat.

In a small saucepan over medium heat, combine the vinegar, bay leaf, oregano, peppercorns, salt, and sugar. Bring to a boil, stirring to dissolve the salt and sugar. Remove from the heat.

Using a slotted spoon, remove the chiles and other vegetables from the skillet and pack into a sterilized 1-pint mason jar. They should be packed tightly all the way to the top. Pour in the vinegar to cover all the vegetables. Let cool and then refrigerate for up to 1 month.

# TEPARY BEAN TACOS

## WITH BUFFALO AND BACON

*Serves 4 to 6*

6 SLICES HIGH-QUALITY BACON, diced

1 SMALL WHITE or YELLOW ONION, finely chopped

1 POUND GROUND BUFFALO

2 TEASPOONS CUMIN SEEDS, toasted and ground (page 29)

½ TEASPOON CAYENNE PEPPER

SALT AND FRESHLY GROUND PEPPER

LARD (page 110) or SUNFLOWER OIL, if needed

12 CORN TORTILLAS

1½ CUPS DRAINED, COOKED TEPARY BEANS (page 23), warmed

ABOUT 1½ CUPS THREE-CHILE SALSA (page 56)

2 AVOCADOS, pitted, peeled, and sliced

½ CUP FRESH CILANTRO LEAVES

ABOUT 2 CUPS SHREDDED ICEBERG LETTUCE

*Using buffalo meat and tepary beans would make this taco unrecognizable in Mexico. Still, these North American ingredients seem right at home stuffed into a corn tortilla. Buffalo is available ground in specialty grocery stores and is a reasonably priced, lower-fat alternative to ground beef. Bacon adds richness to buffalo's leanness. Serve these tacos with "Taco Truck" Pickled Jalapeños and Carrots (facing page).*

In a large, heavy skillet over medium heat, sauté the bacon until all the fat is rendered and the bacon is brown but not crisp, 8 to 10 minutes. Add the onion and sauté until soft and fragrant, about 10 minutes. Add the buffalo, cumin, cayenne, and salt and pepper to taste. Cook until the meat is no longer pink, breaking it up with a large spoon or spatula as it browns, adding a little vegetable oil or lard if the pan seems too dry.

In a small, heavy skillet or *comal* over medium heat, warm each tortilla until soft. Spoon about ⅛ cup of the beans and ¼ cup of the meat mixture onto each tortilla. Top with about 2 tablespoons of the salsa, a few avocado slices, a pinch of cilantro leaves, and some of the lettuce.

Alternatively, serve the tacos family style. Wrap the warm tortillas in a clean kitchen towel and place in a basket. Spoon the beans and meat into separate warmed bowls and put the lettuce, cilantro, and avocado on a platter. Serve the salsa in a separate bowl and let diners assemble their own tacos at the table.

**Substitution Note:** Try Anasazi, Rio Zape, or pinto beans.

# CARNE
## EN SU JUGO

*Serves 4*

**6 SLICES HIGH-QUALITY BACON**, diced

**1 POUND LEAN BEEF** such as sirloin tip or top round, cut against the grain into ¼-inch-thick slices and chopped (see note)

**4 CUPS BEEF BROTH**

**2 CHIPOTLE CHILES IN ADOBO**

**SALT AND FRESHLY GROUND PEPPER**

**2 CUPS DRAINED, COOKED *FLOR DE MAYO* BEANS** (page 23)

**CILANTRO LEAVES** for serving

**LIME WEDGES** for serving

**FINELY CHOPPED GREEN ONIONS**, white and pale green parts, for serving

*There are many versions of this dish, and they all seem to be a thin-broth beef and bacon soup with beans. In Jalisco, the bean of choice is more often than not* mayacoba, *known there as* peruano, *but I like to use* flor de mayo *or pinto.*

In a medium, heavy skillet over medium heat, sauté the bacon until all the fat is rendered and the bacon is brown but not crisp, 8 to 10 minutes. Remove with a slotted spoon and drain on a paper towel–lined plate. Add the beef to the skillet and sauté until brown, turning often with tongs, 2 to 3 minutes. Transfer the beef to a large Dutch oven or other heavy pot.

In a blender, combine 1 cup of the beef broth and the chiles in adobo and blend until smooth. Add to the beef and pour in the remaining beef broth. Season to taste with salt and pepper. Bring to a boil over medium-high heat, reduce the heat to low, and simmer until the meat is tender and the flavors are blended, about 20 minutes.

In a small saucepan over low heat, warm the beans. Ladle them into warmed bowls. Ladle the meat with its broth over the beans. Top with the bacon and cilantro leaves. Pass the lime wedges and green onions at the table.

**Note:** It is easier to slice the meat thinly if you freeze it for about 20 minutes.

**Substitution Note:** Any creamy pintolike bean is great here. Try Anasazi, *flor de junio*, or Rio Zape.

# CUBAN ROAST
# PORK

*Serves 6*

**6 GARLIC CLOVES**, 4 peeled and left whole, 2 peeled and thinly sliced

**2 TEASPOONS COARSE SALT**

**2 TEASPOONS CUMIN SEEDS**, toasted and ground (page 29)

**1 TEASPOON DRIED MEXICAN OREGANO**

**ONE 3-POUND BONELESS PORK SHOULDER**

**JUICE OF 2 GRAPEFRUITS**

**JUICE OF 2 LEMONS**

**JUICE OF 2 LIMES**

**½ LARGE YELLOW ONION**, thinly sliced

**CUBAN BLACK BEANS SOFRITO** (page 113)

*Pork cooked with garlic and citrus until succulent, accompanied with black beans and a mojito, defines Cuban cuisine for me. Perhaps a loaf of moist cassava bread, a full moon, and an empty stomach would make the scene complete. Serve with the Cuban Black Beans Sofrito (page 113) along with some sliced fried plantains. The pork here marinates overnight. If you are making the black beans, you can start cooking the pork and beans at roughly the same time, as each takes 2 to 3 hours but requires very little attention.*

In a mortar with a pestle, mash the 4 whole garlic cloves and coarse salt to a paste. Add the cumin and oregano and mash to combine.

Using a sharp paring knife, cut little slits all over the surface of the pork. Insert the garlic slices into the slits. Rub the garlic paste all over the pork. Put the pork in a glass or ceramic dish and pour the grapefruit, lemon, and lime juices over it. Cover and marinate in the refrigerator overnight, turning once or twice to make sure the entire surface of the pork has been submerged for several hours in the juice.

Preheat oven to 375°F.

Remove the pork from the marinade, reserving the marinade, and pat dry. Put the pork, fat side down, in a Dutch oven or other heavy ovenproof pot. Scatter the onion slices over the pork. Roast, uncovered, for 30 minutes.

In a small saucepan, boil the marinade for at least 10 minutes. Reduce the oven temperature to 325°F. Pour a little of the marinade over the pork and cover the pot with a lid or aluminum foil. Cook until the pork is fork-tender, 2½ to 3 hours. Check the roast every 30 minutes and add a little more of the marinade. Slice the pork and serve with the juices spooned over it and the *sofrito*.

# SANTA MARIA PINQUITOS AND TRI-TIP STEAK

*Serves 6*

## BEANS

**1 POUND SANTA MARIA *PINQUITO* BEANS**, soaked (page 21)

**1 MEDIUM YELLOW** or **WHITE ONION**, chopped

**3 GARLIC CLOVES**, minced

**½ TEASPOON DRY MUSTARD**

**½ TEASPOON SPANISH SMOKED PAPRIKA**

**1 TABLESPOON TOMATO PASTE**

**SALT AND FRESHLY GROUND PEPPER**

---

**5 LARGE GARLIC CLOVES**

**2 TEASPOONS COARSE SALT**

**1 TEASPOON FRESHLY GROUND PEPPER**

**2 TO 2½ POUNDS TRI-TIP**

**CLASSIC RED SALSA** (page 57) or **THREE-CHILE SALSA** (page 56)

*Natives of Santa Maria County in Southern California will tell you that a classic tri-tip barbecue can't be authentic unless it's cooked in Santa Maria over the red oak indigenous to the area, but this version is still a mighty tasty meal. In Santa Maria they'd top the meat with salsa and serve it with garlic bread and a simple salad. This version involves sliced meat, beans, and salsa wrapped up in a tortilla.*

**Make the beans:** Place the beans and their soaking water in a stockpot and add cold water if needed to cover the beans by at least 1 inch. Bring to a boil. Reduce the heat to low and simmer, partially covered, until the beans are beginning to soften, about 1 hour. Add the onion, garlic, mustard, paprika, tomato paste, and salt and pepper to taste. Continue to cook until the beans are tender, about 30 minutes. Taste and adjust the seasonings.

About 30 minutes before serving, prepare a medium-hot fire in a grill, using hardwood if you can.

In a mortar with a pestle, mash the garlic, coarse salt, and pepper to a paste. Rub the garlic paste all over the meat. Put the meat on the rack directly over the hot coals. Grill, turning as needed, until the meat is charred and an instant-read thermometer inserted into the thickest part reads 130°F for rare or 145°F for medium-rare. The thin portion will be cooked more than the thicker portion. Let the meat rest for 10 minutes before slicing it thinly against the grain. Serve with the beans and salsa.

# BORLOTTI BEANS
## IN TOMATO SAUCE WITH CREAMY POLENTA

*Serves 4 to 6*

### TOMATO SAUCE

3 TABLESPOONS UNSALTED BUTTER

½ MEDIUM YELLOW ONION, chopped

1 MEDIUM FENNEL BULB, trimmed and chopped

3 GARLIC CLOVES, finely chopped

4 TEASPOONS CHOPPED FRESH OREGANO

¼ TEASPOON RED PEPPER FLAKES

SALT

1 SMALL CARROT, peeled and shredded

ONE 28-OUNCE CAN WHOLE SAN MARZANO TOMATOES or PLUM TOMATOES

FRESHLY GROUND PEPPER

2 CUPS DRAINED, COOKED *BORLOTTI* BEANS (page 23)

⅓ CUP CHOPPED FRESH FLAT-LEAF PARSLEY

*This is a complete winter's meal. It's hearty and vegetarian, but if you want to include Italian sausage, cook it separately, slice it, and serve on top of the finished dish. For a streamlined process, make the tomato sauce and the beans ahead and heat them together while you cook the polenta.*

**Make the sauce:** In a small Dutch oven or other heavy pot over medium heat, melt the butter. Add the onion, the fennel, the garlic, 2 teaspoons of the oregano, the red pepper flakes, and a pinch of salt. Sauté until the vegetables are soft and fragrant, about 10 minutes. Add the carrot and sauté for 2 to 3 minutes. Add the tomatoes with their juice, stirring to break them up with a wooden spoon. Add another pinch of salt. Reduce the heat to low and cook, uncovered, at the barest simmer, stirring occasionally, until the tomatoes are reduced and beginning to separate from the oil, at least 2 hours or up to 3 hours. Add the remaining 2 teaspoons oregano and salt and pepper to taste. The sauce can be made up to this point 1 or 2 days ahead; let cool and refrigerate.

*continued-*

# BORLOTTI BEANS
## IN TOMATO SAUCE WITH CREAMY POLENTA

*-continued*

### POLENTA

**4 CUPS WATER**

**1 TEASPOON SALT**

**1 CUP POLENTA**

**2 TABLESPOONS UNSALTED BUTTER**

**½ CUP FRESHLY GRATED PARMESAN CHEESE**, plus more for garnishing

**FRESHLY GROUND PEPPER**

**Make the polenta:** About 45 minutes before serving, bring the water to a boil in a medium, heavy-bottomed saucepan. Add the salt and, whisking continuously, slowly pour the polenta into the water in a thin stream. Reduce the heat to low and cook, stirring nearly constantly with a long-handled wooden spoon, until the mixture thickens, the grains soften, and the polenta begins to pull away from the sides of the pan, 40 to 45 minutes. Stir in the butter and ½ cup of the Parmesan, and season with pepper. Cover to keep warm.

Add the beans to the tomato sauce and warm them together over medium-low heat, stirring occasionally. Stir in the parsley about 5 minutes before serving.

Spoon the polenta into warmed shallow bowls and make a well in the center of each serving. Spoon the tomato sauce into the well. Garnish with Parmesan cheese.

**Substitution Note:** This dish is best made with a rich, creamy bean. If *borlotti* are unavailable, try French horticulture, or wren's egg.

# RISOTTO
## AND
# CRANBERRY
# BEANS
## WITH PANCETTA

*Serves 6*

5 CUPS CHICKEN BROTH

2 TABLESPOONS UNSALTED BUTTER

1 TABLESPOON EXTRA-VIRGIN OLIVE OIL

¼ POUND PANCETTA, diced

1 SMALL YELLOW ONION, finely chopped

½ CELERY STALK, finely chopped

2 CUPS ARBORIO or CARNAROLI RICE

½ CUP DRY WHITE WINE

1½ CUPS DRAINED, COOKED CRANBERRY BEANS (page 23), with reserved broth

½ CUP GRATED PARMESAN CHEESE

½ CUP CHOPPED FRESH FLAT-LEAF PARSLEY

SALT AND FRESHLY GROUND PEPPER

*Cranberry beans stand out as one of the best. Every member of the entire family of beans—from tongues of fire to borlotti— has a creamy, velvety texture and superb pot liquor. That's why you often see the bean in dishes like pasta e fagioli. Less common but equally wonderful is Italy's version of beans and rice. The gorgeous bean broth bathes each grain of rice, making a perfect dish on its own or as an accompaniment to roasted pork or grilled chops. The unmistakable peppery-savory flavor of pancetta is perfect here, but if you prefer a pork-free dish, it's delicious without.*

In a medium saucepan over medium heat, bring the broth to a simmer. Adjust the heat to maintain the barest simmer as you prepare the risotto.

In a large, heavy skillet over medium heat, melt the butter with the olive oil. Add the pancetta and onion and sauté until golden brown and fragrant, about 10 minutes. Add the celery and sauté for 2 to 3 minutes. Add the rice and stir to coat thoroughly. Raise the heat to medium-high, pour in the wine, and cook, stirring briskly, until absorbed. Add the broth ½ cup at a time, stirring constantly, and making sure each addition of broth is absorbed before adding more.

Total cooking time should be about 40 minutes, depending on the pan and level of heat. Begin tasting the grains of rice after about 20 minutes to assess doneness. When it is done, the rice should be creamy with a bit of bite in the middle, but not chalky. You may not use all the broth or you may need more. If you need more, dilute the remaining broth with a little water, keeping it warm.

When the rice is just short of done and only 1 or 2 additions of broth remain, add the cranberry beans and ½ cup of their broth and stir into the rice to warm thoroughly. Add more chicken broth and check the rice for doneness again. When the rice is done, turn off the heat and stir in the Parmesan and parsley and season with salt and pepper.

# PASTA
## WITH
# BEANS,
## BROCCOLI RABE,
## AND BACON

*Serves 4*

**3 SLICES HIGH-QUALITY BACON**, cut crosswise into
¼-inch-thick strips

**2 TABLESPOONS EXTRA-VIRGIN OLIVE OIL**, plus more for
serving

**2 GARLIC CLOVES**, finely chopped

**1 SMALL FENNEL BULB**, trimmed and cut into ¼-inch dice

**2 BUNCHES BROCCOLI RABE**, tough stems trimmed and
chopped (about 2 cups)

**1 CUP DRAINED, COOKED RUNNER CANNELLINI, *CELLINI*, or
MARROW BEANS** (page 23), with reserved broth

**½ POUND SHORT TUBULAR PASTA** such as penne, rigatoni,
or *gemelli*

**¼ TO ½ TEASPOON DRIED RED PEPPER FLAKES** (optional)

**SALT AND FRESHLY GROUND PEPPER**

**¼ CUP TOASTED BREAD CRUMBS**

**¼ CUP FRESHLY GRATED PARMESAN CHEESE**, plus more for
serving

*Here's an easy recipe that you can quickly assemble anytime
you have a cup of cooked white beans and a few odds and ends
in your refrigerator. You can substitute chard or kale for the
broccoli rabe or use cabbage or regular broccoli. Among other
options, you can leave out the fennel or use leeks instead or
omit the bacon or use sausage instead.*

Bring a large pot of water to boil and salt it generously.

In a large, heavy skillet over medium heat, sauté the bacon until the
fat is rendered and the bacon is brown and beginning to crisp, 8 to
10 minutes. Using a slotted spoon, remove bacon to a paper towel–
lined plate. Pour off most of the fat from the pan, add the 2 tablespoons of olive oil, and warm over medium heat. Sauté the garlic
and fennel until vegetables are soft and wilted, about 10 minutes.

Add the broccoli rabe and sauté until coated and beginning to wilt.
Add a splash of the reserved bean broth and cook, stirring to scrape
up the browned bits from the bottom of the pan. Cover partially
and cook, stirring occasionally, until the broccoli rabe is tender
and wilted, about 10 minutes.

Meanwhile, cook the pasta according to the package instructions
until it is al dente. Drain the pasta but do not rinse.

When the broccoli rabe is cooked, add the pasta, beans, reserved
bacon, and more bean broth if the mixture seems dry. Add the red
pepper flakes (if using) and salt and pepper to taste. Toss well.

Remove from the heat and add the bread crumbs and the ¼ cup
Parmesan. Toss and serve in warmed bowls. Top each serving with a
drizzle of olive oil, more Parmesan, and freshly ground pepper.

# SKEWERS OF SWORDFISH, SHRIMP, AND TOMATOES ON

# BLACK CALYPSO BEANS

*Serves 4*

---

1 TEASPOON CHOPPED FRESH ROSEMARY

2 TEASPOONS GRATED LEMON ZEST

2 GENEROUS PINCHES OF RED PEPPER FLAKES

6 GARLIC CLOVES, finely chopped

⅔ CUP PLUS 3 TABLESPOONS EXTRA-VIRGIN OLIVE OIL

2 TEASPOONS RED WINE VINEGAR

SALT AND FRESHLY GROUND PEPPER

1 POUND SWORDFISH, cut into 1-inch cubes

1 TABLESPOON CHOPPED FRESH CHIVES

1 TABLESPOON CHOPPED FRESH MINT

1½ TABLESPOONS CHOPPED FRESH OREGANO

4 TABLESPOONS FRESH LEMON JUICE

*There's something primal and fun about cooking food on a stick. It's pretty basic, practical, and easy enough to do. If you have a rosemary plant, clip four straight, sturdy branches, strip off the leaves, and use these branches as skewers for the swordfish. If not, just use all bamboo skewers.*

Soak 8 bamboo skewers in water.

In a medium bowl, whisk together the rosemary, the lemon zest, the pepper flakes, one-third of the minced garlic, ⅓ cup of the olive oil, and the vinegar. Season with salt and pepper. Put the swordfish cubes in a shallow glass or ceramic dish and pour the oil mixture over them. Toss to coat and marinate in the refrigerator for 30 to 45 minutes.

In a medium bowl, whisk together the chives, the mint, the oregano, the lemon juice, one-third of the minced garlic, and ⅓ cup of the olive oil. Season with salt and pepper. Put the shrimp in a shallow glass or ceramic dish and pour the mixture over them. Toss to coat and marinate in the refrigerator for 30 to 45 minutes.

In a large, heavy skillet over medium heat, warm the 3 tablespoons olive oil. Sauté the chopped onion and remaining garlic until soft and fragrant, about 10 minutes. Add the wine and cook until nearly evaporated. Add the beans and the mixed herbs. Warm gently and adjust the seasonings with salt and pepper. Keep warm.

Preheat the broiler or prepare a charcoal grill or gas grill for grilling over medium heat.

**12 LARGE SHRIMP**, peeled and deveined

**½ CUP FINELY CHOPPED YELLOW ONION**

**⅔ CUP DRY WHITE WINE**

**3 CUPS PARTIALLY DRAINED, COOKED BLACK CALYPSO BEANS** (page 23)

**1 TABLESPOON CHOPPED MIXED HERBS** such as rosemary, chives, oregano, and mint

**ABOUT 24 SMALL GRAPE** or **CHERRY TOMATOES**

**LEMON WEDGES** for serving

Thread the swordfish cubes onto 4 bamboo skewers, dividing them evenly.

Thread the shrimp and cherry tomatoes onto the remaining 4 skewers, alternating the shrimp and tomatoes.

Line a baking sheet with aluminum foil and place the skewers on top. Broil, turning once with tongs, for 2 to 3 minutes per side. Alternatively, put the skewers on the grill rack and grill for about the same amount of time. The shrimp should be pink, firm, and opaque, and the swordfish should be white, firm, and opaque.

Spoon about ¾ cup of beans onto each plate. Put 1 swordfish skewer and 1 shrimp skewer on the beans and serve with lemon wedges on the side.

LORNA SASS'S

# SCARLET RUNNER BEANS

## WITH FARRO RISOTTO AND SAFFRON

*Serves 4*

½ TEASPOON SAFFRON THREADS

1 TABLESPOON WARM WATER

1 TABLESPOON PLUS 1 TEASPOON EXTRA-VIRGIN OLIVE OIL

½ MEDIUM YELLOW ONION, chopped

1¼ CUPS SEMIPEARLED *FARRO*

⅓ CUP DRY WHITE WINE, VERMOUTH, or SHERRY

3 TO 3½ CUPS CHICKEN or VEGETABLE BROTH

1½ CUPS DRAINED, COOKED SCARLET RUNNER BEANS (page 23)

⅓ CUP FRESHLY GRATED PARMESAN CHEESE, plus more for garnishing

½ CUP COARSELY CHOPPED TOASTED WALNUTS

1 TEASPOON MINCED FRESH LEMON THYME or ROSEMARY

SALT AND FRESHLY GROUND PEPPER

*From the moment I met Lorna Sass, I felt as if I were visiting with an old friend. Lorna's pressure cooker books are seminal, and I'd always been interested in what she wrote. As her recipe shows, risotto is one of the dishes that the pressure cooker does best. The cooker pulls the starch out of the grain in record time so you need only stir for a few moments to finish off the dish rather than stand at the stove during the entire cooking time. Farro, a type of emmer wheat, is an ancient cousin of the wheat commonly grown in this country. The starch in farro creates a wonderfully creamy risotto. Italian farro is sold in most gourmet shops and is readily available by mail order. For this dish, you'll need semipearled farro, labeled farro pelato. If you don't have farro on hand, see the variation that uses rice.*

Using a mortar and pestle, crush the saffron threads and stir in the warm water. Alternatively, crush in a small bowl with a spoon. Set aside.

In a 4-quart (or larger) pressure cooker over medium-high heat, warm the oil. Sauté the onions until they begin to soften, 2 to 3 minutes. Add the *farro* and stir to coat with the oil. Continue cooking and stirring until the *farro* releases a toasted aroma, about 2 minutes. Stir in the wine and cook until it evaporates. Stir in 3 cups of the chicken broth, stirring to scrape up any browned bits sticking to the bottom of the cooker.

Lock the lid in place. Bring to high pressure over high heat. Reduce the heat just enough to maintain high pressure and cook for 8 minutes. Turn off the heat. Quick-release the pressure according to the manufacturer's instructions. Remove the lid, tilting it away from you to allow steam to escape.

*continued-*

LORNA SASS'S
# SCARLET RUNNER BEANS
## WITH FARRO RISOTTO AND SAFFRON

*-continued*

Stir in the saffron. Set the cooker over medium-high heat and stir the *farro* vigorously. Boil uncovered, stirring every minute or so, until the mixture thickens and the *farro* is tender but still chewy, 1 to 3 minutes. If the mixture becomes dry before the *farro* is done, stir in ¼ to ½ cup of the remaining broth. The finished risotto should be slightly runny; it will continue to thicken as it sits on the plate.

Stir in the scarlet runner beans and cook for 1 minute. Turn off the heat and stir in the ⅓ cup cheese, walnuts, and thyme. Add salt and pepper to taste. Serve in shallow bowls or on plates. Garnish each portion with additional cheese.

**Rice Variation:** Substitute 1½ cups Arborio or Carnaroli rice for the *farro*. Increase the broth to 3½ to 4 cups. Decrease the cooking time under pressure to 4 minutes.

**Substitution Note:** You can use marrow beans, but the color of the scarlet runners against the saffron is fabulous.

# SEAFOOD AND YELLOW EYE BEAN STEW
## WITH SAFFRON

*Serves 4 to 5*

1 TEASPOON SAFFRON THREADS

1 TABLESPOON WARM WATER

3 TABLESPOONS EXTRA-VIRGIN OLIVE OIL

1 MEDIUM FENNEL BULB, trimmed and cut into
⅛-inch-thick slices

2 GARLIC CLOVES, thinly sliced

1 CUP DRY WHITE WINE

1 CUP CANNED DICED TOMATOES

1 CUP WATER

1½ POUNDS MANILA CLAMS

½ POUND MEDIUM-LARGE SHRIMP, heads intact, unpeeled

1 POUND MILD WHITE FISH FILLETS such as snapper or
sole, cut into 2-inch chunks

SALT AND FRESHLY GROUND PEPPER

1½ CUPS DRAINED, COOKED YELLOW EYE BEANS (page 23;
cooked with the addition of 1 bay leaf)

¼ CUP CHOPPED FRESH FLAT-LEAF PARSLEY

*Yellow eye beans are famous as the perfect partner to a ham hock. That's well and good, but limiting them to an occasional winter stew would be a mistake. They have a gorgeous soft texture that works well in stews and with seafood. This variation on Mediterranean seafood stew comes together quickly once the beans are cooked. Accompany with crusty bread.*

Using a mortar and pestle, crush the saffron threads and stir in the warm water. Alternatively, crush in a small bowl with a spoon. Set aside.

In a large Dutch oven or other heavy pot with a lid over medium heat, warm the olive oil. Sauté the fennel until soft and golden, about 5 minutes. Add the garlic; sauté for 1 to 2 minutes. Add the wine, tomatoes with their juice, water, and saffron. Bring to a simmer, add the clams (discarding any that do not close to the touch), cover, and cook until most of the clams are open, 3 to 4 minutes.

Add the shrimp, fish, a little salt, and a generous amount of pepper, and stir gently to make sure all of the seafood is mostly submerged in liquid. Add a little more water if neccessary. Cover the pan tightly and cook, stirring gently one time to make sure the seafood cooks evenly, until the fish is perfectly opaque and the shrimp are pink and opaque throughout, 5 to 6 minutes. Remove from the heat and discard any unopened clams. Add the beans and parsley and heat through, tossing very gently to avoid breaking up the fish. Taste and adjust the seasonings. Serve in warmed shallow bowls.

**Substitution Note:** Any mild white bean such as cannellini or marrow will work well in this dish, as would flageolet beans.

# MARROW BEANS
## WITH PANFRIED FISH, ANCHOVY BUTTER, AND EGGS

*Serves 4*

**ANCHOVY BUTTER**

**2 LARGE GARLIC CLOVES**

**COARSE SALT**

**4 OIL-PACKED ANCHOVY FILLETS,** or **2 SALT-PACKED ANCHOVIES,** cleaned (page 29)

**4 TABLESPOONS UNSALTED BUTTER, AT ROOM TEMPERATURE**

**FRESHLY GROUND PEPPER**

*When I first heard about marrow beans, I was told to prepare myself for their bacon flavor. I was so disappointed that I couldn't taste bacon that I never really gave these beans much thought. Slowly, I noticed good cooks gravitating toward marrow beans, and because in some ways I'm a born follower, I got on board, and now they're one of my favorites. Unlike white runner beans, which are buttery, and* gigandes *beans, which are somewhat like a potato, marrows are light—perfect for this fish dish. As a Bay Area native, I prefer to make it with sand dabs.*

**Make the anchovy butter:** In a mortar with a pestle, pound the garlic with a small pinch of coarse salt until the garlic is smashed. Add the anchovies and pound until a smooth paste forms. In a small bowl, blend the softened butter with the anchovy-garlic paste. Add pepper to taste and set aside.

½ **POUND MARROW BEANS**, cooked (page 23) and partially drained.

4 **MILD WHITE FISH FILLETS** such as sole, sand dabs, or snapper, about 1 pound total

½ **CUP ALL-PURPOSE FLOUR**

1 **TEASPOON SALT**

½ **TEASPOON FRESHLY GROUND PEPPER**

2 **TO 3 TABLESPOONS UNSALTED BUTTER**

1 **BUNCH ARUGULA**, tough stems removed

3 **TABLESPOONS CHOPPED FRESH FLAT-LEAF PARSLEY**

4 **EGGS**

In a small saucepan over low heat, warm the beans. Preheat the oven to 200°F.

Rinse the fish fillets and pat dry. Combine the flour, salt, and pepper on a plate. In a large, heavy skillet over medium-high heat, melt 1 tablespoon of the butter. Dredge the fish fillets in the flour mixture, shaking them gently to remove any excess flour. Cook the fish fillets 2 at a time, turning carefully with a spatula, until they begin to brown and become opaque throughout, 2 to 3 minutes per side. Transfer to a plate and keep warm in the oven. You may need to add more butter to the pan to cook the second batch of fillets.

When all the fillets are cooked, add half of the anchovy butter to the warm beans and toss to combine. Remove from heat and transfer to a large bowl. Toss the arugula and parsley in the beans to wilt slightly.

Working quickly, in a medium nonstick skillet over medium-low heat, melt the remaining 1 tablespoon of butter. Fry the eggs, 2 at a time, over easy, 2 to 3 minutes. Season the eggs with salt and pepper.

While you fry the eggs, begin assembling the plates, 2 at a time, covering the finished plates to keep them warm. Spoon about 1 cup of the beans onto each plate. Drape a fish fillet over the beans. Drape a fried egg opposite the fillet. Dot each fillet with some of the remaining anchovy butter.

**Substitution Note:** Use *cellini*, runner cannellini, or flageolet beans.

# MARROW BEANS

## WITH MERGUEZ SAUSAGE, PISTACHIOS, AND HONEY

*Serves 4*

½ **POUND MARROW BEANS**, soaked (page 21)

1 **TEASPOON EXTRA-VIRGIN OLIVE OIL**

1 **POUND FRESH *MERGUEZ* SAUSAGE**

½ **MEDIUM YELLOW ONION**, chopped

3 **GARLIC CLOVES**, finely chopped

1 **CELERY STALK**, chopped

1 **TEASPOON CORIANDER SEEDS**, toasted and ground (page 29)

½ **TEASPOON CUMIN SEEDS**, toasted and ground (page 29)

2 **TEASPOONS ALEPPO PEPPER**

**SALT**

1 **BUNCH CHARD** or **COLLARD GREENS**, tough stems removed and cut into ribbons

1 **CUP CHOPPED FRESH FLAT-LEAF PARSLEY**

2 **TEASPOONS GRATED LEMON ZEST**

1 **TABLESPOON LEMON JUICE**

2 **TEASPOONS *HARISSA* PASTE**

**FRESHLY GROUND PEPPER**

⅓ **CUP CHOPPED PISTACHIOS** for garnishing

2 **TO 3 TEASPOONS HONEY** for garnishing

*Sausages and legumes are a marriage made in heaven, but happily available locally. This recipe obviously is influenced by North Africa, with its earthy merguez sausages made from lamb, exotic pistachios, and drizzle of honey. Aleppo pepper is a Syrian pepper with a fruity, savory heat that blends well with the earthiness of the lamb. If you're having difficulty finding lamb sausage, try www.fattedcalf.com.*

In a medium saucepan over medium-high heat, bring the beans and their soaking water to a boil.

In a large, heavy skillet over medium heat, warm the olive oil. Add the sausages and cook, turning frequently, until browned and just cooked through, 5 to 7 minutes. Remove to paper towels to drain. Refrigerate until serving.

Pour off most of the fat from the skillet and set over medium heat. Add the onion, garlic, and celery and sauté, stirring and scraping up the browned bits from the bottom of the pan. Add a little water if needed to loosen the browned bits and keep the vegetables from sticking. Cook the vegetables until soft, about 10 minutes.

Add the vegetables, coriander, cumin, and Aleppo pepper to the beans. Partially cover and simmer until the beans begin to soften, about 1 hour. Season with salt and continue to cook until the beans are soft, about 30 minutes.

In a small, heavy skillet over low heat, gently warm the sausages.

Add the greens to the beans and cook, stirring, until tender. Remove from heat and stir in the parsley, lemon zest and juice, and *harissa* paste. Add salt and pepper to taste. Serve the beans in warmed shallow bowls. Slice the sausage and arrange on the beans. Sprinkle with the pistachios and drizzle with the honey.

**Substitution Note:** Use *cellini*, runner cannellini, or flageolet beans.

# FLAGEOLET BEAN AND HALIBUT STEW

## WITH ASPARAGUS AND PARSLEY-MINT PISTOU

*Serves 4*

3 TABLESPOONS EXTRA-VIRGIN OLIVE OIL

2 GARLIC CLOVES

1 CELERY STALK, chopped

½ MEDIUM YELLOW ONION, chopped

½ POUND FLAGEOLET BEANS, soaked (page 21)

SALT AND FRESHLY GROUND PEPPER

1½ POUNDS HALIBUT, cut into 2-inch pieces

1 LARGE BUNCH ASPARAGUS, tough ends trimmed and cut into bite-size pieces

3 STEMS GREEN GARLIC, sliced lengthwise (optional)

⅓ CUP TOASTED BREAD CRUMBS

### PISTOU

1 GARLIC CLOVE

SALT

½ CUP FRESH FLAT-LEAF PARSLEY LEAVES

⅓ CUP FRESH MINT LEAVES

2 TABLESPOONS EXTRA-VIRGIN OLIVE OIL

*Matching fish and beans wouldn't be my first instinct, but the more I play around with the combination, the more I enjoy it. Since both have somewhat mild flavors, the asparagus and pistou are key to this savory dish. If you cannot find green garlic, the stew is still delicious without it. And if your broiler will not accommodate a Dutch oven, warm the bread crumbs with a bit of olive oil in a skillet and sprinkle on the stew before serving.*

In a large Dutch oven or other heavy ovenproof pot over medium heat, warm 2 tablespoons of the olive oil. Sauté the garlic, celery, and onion until soft and fragrant, about 10 minutes. Add the flageolets and their soaking water, and more cold water if needed to cover the beans by 1 inch. Bring to a boil, reduce the heat to low, and simmer gently until the beans are almost tender, about 1 hour. Season with salt and pepper to taste and continue to cook until the beans are soft, about 30 minutes.

Make the *pistou*: Put the garlic in a mortar or small food processor. Add a pinch of salt and grind to a paste with a pestle or process until finely chopped. Add the parsley and mint and grind or process until finely chopped. Add the olive oil and grind or process until the oil and herbs are well blended. Set aside.

Preheat the broiler. Add the halibut, asparagus, and green garlic (if using) to the beans, distributing the ingredients evenly and pushing them down with a wooden spoon to submerge them partially. Simmer gently, carefully turning the fish pieces once, until the halibut is cooked through and the asparagus is tender, 10 to 15 minutes. Do not stir, as you don't want to break up the fish pieces. Sprinkle the bread crumbs evenly over the stew and drizzle with the remaining 1 tablespoon oil. Put under the broiler and cook until the stew is bubbly and the bread crumbs are browned.

Serve the stew in warmed shallow bowls and garnish each portion with *pistou*.

**Substitution Note:** Flageolet beans are very distinct and have no substitute. If they are unavailable, use a mild white bean.

# PRATHER RANCH

# SPRING LAMB AND FLAGEOLETS

## WITH FAY'S RELISH

*Serves 6*

**2 TABLESPOONS EXTRA-VIRGIN OLIVE OIL**, plus more if needed

**2 POUNDS BONE-IN LAMB SHOULDER STEAKS**

**SALT AND FRESHLY GROUND PEPPER**

**2 SMALL CARROTS,** peeled and chopped

**1 CELERY STALK**, chopped

**½ MEDIUM YELLOW ONION**, chopped

**3 GARLIC CLOVES**, finely chopped

**1 POUND FLAGEOLET BEANS**, soaked (page 21)

*I used to work seven days a week, running from the fields to the warehouse to the farmers' markets and back. I had a new business and knew I was paying some dues. The bright spot was at one of the markets, where I was next to Doug Stonebreaker of Prather Ranch Meat Co., who seemed to be working the same seven days a week I was. Our market day together was as close to a social life as I got. Doug and I would trade marketing ideas and recipes and plan for bigger days. Prather Ranch is now famous for being a forerunner in the organic and humane meat business.*

*Every spring, Doug, his wife, and some friends have a party at my place to remember what working seven days a week was like. We always cook this dish in a clay pot and serve it with our lovely friend Fay's relish, which she calls "Cilantro Gremolata or Something of the Sort." I just call it "Fay's Relish" and use it on almost everything.*

In a large Dutch oven or other heavy pot over medium-high heat, warm the olive oil. Season the lamb generously with salt and pepper. Working in batches, add the lamb to the pot and cook, turning once, until well browned on both sides, about 3 minutes per side. Remove to a plate.

Reduce the heat to medium and add the carrots, celery, onion, and garlic and stir to scrape up the browned bits from the bottom of the pan. Add more oil if the vegetables stick and a splash of water to help release the browned bits.

Add the beans and their soaking water to the pot and add more cold water if needed to cover the beans by 1 inch. Return the lamb with its juice to the pot. Bring to a boil, skimming off any impurities that rise to the top, and cook for 5 minutes. Reduce the heat to low and simmer slowly until the beans and lamb are tender, 1½ to 2 hours.

*continued-*

PRATHER RANCH

# SPRING LAMB AND FLAGEOLETS

## WITH FAY'S RELISH

*-continued*

### FAY'S RELISH

**1 LARGE BUNCH CILANTRO**, chopped

**1 MEDIUM SHALLOT**, minced

**2 GARLIC CLOVES**, minced

**GRATED ZEST OF 1 LEMON**

**JUICE OF ½ LEMON**

**1 TABLESPOON EXTRA-VIRGIN OLIVE OIL**

**Make the relish:** In a small bowl, stir together the cilantro, shallot, garlic, lemon zest and juice, and olive oil.

Remove the lamb from the pot and cut into bite-sized pieces, trimming off excess fat and removing the bones. If you prefer a thicker stew, transfer 1 cup of beans and broth to a blender or food processor and purée until smooth and return to the pot. Return the lamb to the pot, stir, and season to taste with salt and pepper. Cook for an additional 10 minutes and adjust the seasonings.

Serve in warmed shallow bowls and garnish with the relish.

**Substitution Note:** If you can't find flageolet beans, *cellini* or runner cannellini beans will make a nice lamb stew.

# MARROW BEANS
## WITH CLAMS AND CHORIZO

*Serves 4*

3 TABLESPOONS EXTRA-VIRGIN OLIVE OIL

3 STEMS GREEN GARLIC, chopped, or 2 garlic cloves, chopped

3 OUNCES DRY SPANISH CHORIZO, diced

2½ POUNDS MANILA CLAMS

1½ CUPS DRY WHITE or ROSÉ WINE

½ CUP CHOPPED FRESH FLAT-LEAF PARSLEY

2 CUPS DRAINED, COOKED MARROW BEANS (page 23)

FRESHLY GROUND PEPPER

*In Spain, you can find* alubia *beans for dishes like this. The American marrow bean is a close second. In fact, given the choice, I think I'd go for the marrows. They hold their shape and yet they're known for absorbing all the flavors you add. This dish is great with a dry rosé, which you can use for cooking.*

In a large Dutch oven or a soup pot with a lid over medium heat, warm the olive oil. Sauté the garlic until fragrant but not browned, 2 to 3 minutes. Add the chorizo and sauté for 3 to 4 minutes. Add the clams (discarding any that do not close to the touch) and stir to coat. Pour in the wine, cover, raise the heat to medium-high, and cook, shaking the pan occasionally, until the clams open, 7 to 8 minutes. Discard any unopened clams. Add the parsley, beans, and pepper to taste, and toss gently.

Serve in warmed shallow bowls.

**Substitution Note:** Use any white bean, such as *cellini*, cannellini, or white navy beans.

CAKEBREAD CELLARS'

# GOOD MOTHER STALLARD BEAN

## AND CHICKEN POT PIE

*Serves 6*

---

**2 TABLESPOONS EXTRA-VIRGIN OLIVE OIL**

**2 POUNDS SKINLESS, BONELESS CHICKEN THIGHS**, cut into 1-inch pieces

**SALT AND FRESHLY GROUND PEPPER**

**1 SMALL YELLOW ONION**, chopped

**1 MEDIUM CARROT**, peeled and finely chopped

**1 CELERY STALK**, finely chopped

**1 TEASPOON TOMATO PASTE**

**1 CUP DRY WHITE WINE**

**1 TEASPOON FRESH THYME LEAVES**

**1 BAY LEAF**

**2 CUPS CHICKEN BROTH**

**2 BUNCHES DINOSAUR KALE**, tough stems removed and roughly chopped

**½ POUND GOOD MOTHER STALLARD** or **CRANBERRY BEANS**, cooked (page 23; cooked with the addition of 1 bay leaf) and cooled in their broth

**ALL-PURPOSE FLOUR** for dusting

**½ POUND FROZEN PUFF PASTRY SHEETS**, thawed for several hours in refrigerator

**1 EGG**, beaten

---

*One of the best parties in the Napa Valley each fall is the American Harvest Workshop at Cakebread Cellars. The Cakebread family and chef Brian Streeter host a flock of chefs, journalists, food producers, and hardcore fans of Cakebread wines for a multiday event that is essentially a boot camp focusing on food and wine pairing. Culminating the event are two dinners featuring the food developed at the workshop, and* breathtaking *is the word that first comes to mind when I think about these dinners.*

*I'm lucky enough to be the "bean guy" at the workshop, but I'm also fortunate in that Brian is a big supporter of beans. I make deliveries year-round, and this recipe is one of the results. Brian makes the rich pot pie with duck legs. By all means use them if you have access to them. You can make one large pie or individual servings. I recommend Cakebread Cellars Syrah as an accompaniment.*

Preheat the oven to 350°F.

In a large Dutch oven or other heavy ovenproof pot over high heat, warm the olive oil. Season the chicken generously with salt and pepper. Working in batches to avoid crowding, add the chicken to the pot and cook, turning carefully with tongs, until evenly browned, about 5 minutes. Remove the chicken to a platter. Reduce the heat to medium-high, add the onion, carrot, and celery and sauté until soft and fragrant, about 10 minutes. Add the tomato paste and white wine, stirring and scraping to loosen any browned bits from the bottom of the pot. Cook at a brisk simmer until the wine is almost evaporated. Return the chicken to the pot and add the thyme, bay leaf, and chicken broth. Cover, transfer to the oven, and cook until the chicken is tender, about 45 minutes.

*continued-*

CAKEBREAD CELLARS'
## GOOD MOTHER STALLARD BEAN AND
# CHICKEN POT PIE

*-continued*

Meanwhile, bring a medium saucepan of water to a boil. Add the kale and cook until wilted, 3 or 4 minutes. Drain and rinse under cold running water. Set aside.

In a blender or food processor, purée 1 cup of the beans and their broth to make a smooth purée. Add to the pot with the chicken along with the remaining beans. Squeeze any excess water from the kale and add to the pot. Stir, return to the oven, and cook for 15 minutes to blend the flavors. Taste and adjust the seasonings.

Remove the chicken and beans from the oven. If making 1 large pot pie, leave the chicken and beans in the pot. If making individual pies, ladle the stew into 6 ramekins or other baking dishes. Raise the oven temperature to 400°F.

Dust a work surface with flour. Roll out the pastry until ⅛ inch thick. Cut a round 1 inch larger than the diameter of the pot or cut out 6 smaller rounds 1 inch larger than the diameter of the baking dishes.

Lightly brush the rim of the pot or the rims of the baking dishes with the beaten egg. Drape the pastry round(s) over the pot or baking dishes and press to seal around the edges. Brush the pastry with the beaten egg. Set the pot or baking dishes on a baking sheet to catch any drips. Bake until the pastry is golden brown, 10 to 12 minutes.

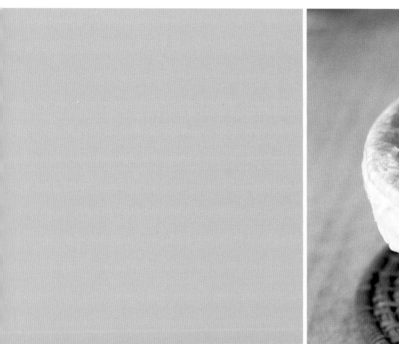

# CARNEROS INN'S
# CHRISTMAS LIMA
## WITH PORK CHOPS, CABBAGE, AND ASIAN PEAR RELISH

*Serves 4*

**3 SLICES HIGH-QUALITY BACON**, diced

**1 TABLESPOON PLUS 1 TEASPOON EXTRA-VIRGIN OLIVE OIL**

**1 SMALL CARROT**, peeled and cut into ¼-inch dice

**½ CUP FINELY CHOPPED YELLOW ONION**

**¼ ANCHO CHILE**, seeded and torn into pieces

**5 GARLIC CLOVES**, finely chopped

**1 BAY LEAF**

**½ POUND CHRISTMAS LIMA BEANS**, soaked (page 21)

**SALT AND FRESHLY GROUND PEPPER**

**1 ASIAN** or **BOSC PEAR**, peeled and cut into ⅛-inch dice

**½ TEASPOON FRESH LEMON JUICE**

**1 TABLESPOON SNIPPED FRESH CHIVES**

**FOUR 10- TO 12-OUNCE BONE-IN PORK CHOPS**

**½ SMALL HEAD SAVOY CABBAGE**, cored and very thinly sliced

*Christmas lima beans are meaty without being too starchy, and they have a good pot liquor. They're also known as chestnut limas because of their flavor. When chef Kimball Jones opened Farm restaurant at the Carneros Inn, almost all the reviews mentioned his pork chops, and they also never failed to mention the beans!*

In a soup pot over medium heat, sauté the bacon until the fat is rendered and the bacon is just starting to brown, 8 to 10 minutes. Pour off all but 2 tablespoons of the fat in the pot. Add the 1 tablespoon olive oil, carrot, and onion. Cook, stirring often, until the vegetables are soft and fragrant, about 10 minutes.

Add the chile, garlic, bay leaf, and beans with their soaking water to the pot. Add more cold water if needed to cover the beans by 1 inch. Bring to a boil and boil vigorously for 10 minutes. Reduce the heat to low and simmer, partially covered, until the beans are tender, about 1 hour. Season to taste with salt and pepper.

Meanwhile, in a glass or ceramic bowl, stir together the pear and lemon juice. Season with salt and pepper. Stir in the chives. Set aside.

Preheat the oven to 400°F or prepare a charcoal grill or gas grill for grilling over medium-high heat.

Season the pork chops with salt and pepper. In a large, heavy, ovenproof skillet over medium-high heat, warm the 1 teaspoon olive oil. Add the pork chops and sear, turning once, until browned, about 3 minutes per side. Transfer the pan to the oven and cook until an instant-read thermometer inserted into the thickest part of the chop reads 140°F for medium or 160°F for well done. Alternatively, put the chops on the grill rack and grill for 8 minutes per side.

*continued-*

CARNEROS INN'S

# CHRISTMAS LIMA
## WITH PORK CHOPS, CABBAGE, AND ASIAN PEAR RELISH

*-continued*

Meanwhile, add the cabbage to the beans, stir gently, and cook until the cabbage is wilted.

Divide the beans and cabbage among 4 plates. Top each portion with a pork chop and garnish with the pear relish.

**Substitution Note:** Any sturdy bean will work here, such as Good Mother Stallard beans, or French horticulture or one of the other cranberry beans.

# ACKNOWLEDGMENTS

### Steve Sando

First and foremost I want to thank the team at Chronicle Books for being so patient and helpful in creating a really wonderful book. My editor, Bill LeBlond, and project manager, Amy Treadwell, brought out the best in everyone and I couldn't be happier.

More big, fat thanks to Katherine Cowles, my super agent, who makes things happen with humor and grace; Vanessa Barrington, whose creative hands produced so many of the good recipes in the book; and Sara Remington, whose photographs bring all the good food to life. I'd also like to thank Alain Capretz for being such a good ear and for introducing me to Sara's photography.

Thanks to Carrie Brown, a stylist and friend that no author should be without.

Thanks to my family, Mary Lee Sando, Suzanne DeWit, Robert and Nico, and my brother Mike. They put up with me and have stories to tell.

Joan Taramasso makes Rancho Gordo possible. It's fruitless to try and thank her for all she does, but I'll try anyway.

Also deserving my gratitude are Karen Schuppert for her dietary information; Christopher Ann Cowen and Susan Fekety, my travel companions; my fellow members of the Family Farm League; my friends at mouthfulsfood.com; the staff at CUESA (especially Dexter and Lulu who make it all happen); and all the great chefs who have discovered the joys of heirloom beans and paid their bills within 30 days.

Thanks also to Jane Connors, Doug Stonebreaker, Julie Brown, Glen Fishman, Eileen and Rich Pharo, Maureen and Mike Crumly, Lucy Gore, Paula Wolfert, Annie Sommerville, Deborah Madison, Lynn Ingersoll, Scott Kraft and the staff of Six Apart, Chip Morris, Candy Rowan, Lassa Skinner, Tony Bogar, Joe Schirmer, Eric Zielbold, and Rachel Lauden.

Last but not least, the biggest thank you to all my growers. Obviously you are the key to the whole thing!

### Vanessa Barrington

I'd like to thank my agent, Kitty Cowles, for her idea to bring Steve Sando and me together to write this book and for guiding us through the proposal process. I thank Steve for growing, finding, and promoting the beans and writing such wonderful stories. Bill LeBlond and Amy Treadwell from Chronicle Books deserve special appreciation for their expert guidance. Thanks to Sara Remington for the perfect photos. Thanks to Carrie Brown whose styling made them shine and for teaching me so much of what I know about cooking and life.

For their help on this book in so many ways: testing or sharing recipes, reading proposals, taking photos, eating their weight in beans, offering advice, simply listening, or all of the above, I thank Bailey Foster, Marcia Tobin, Sue Rochman, Robin Romdalvik, Dan Glover, Debra Resnik, Christina Sunley, Cynthia Wheeler, Shelly Puri, John Ingle, Mary Burger, Marjorie Breyer, Bettemie Prins, Elizabeth Lawton, Elizabeth Crane, Haven Bourque, Erica Sweetman, Jennifer Dobrowolski, and my sisters, Vicki Rogers and Valerie Long. I thank Olivette Rogers for sharing her passion for food with me. She started me on this path. And I thank Susan Fleming for her love, encouragement, and support throughout this process and every day, and for gamely eating whatever is on the menu.

# INDEX

# TABLE OF
# EQUIVALENTS

*The exact equivalents in the following tables have*
*been rounded for convenience.*

## Oven Temperature

| FAHRENHEIT | CELSIUS | GAS |
|---|---|---|
| 250 | 120 | 1/2 |
| 275 | 140 | 1 |
| 300 | 150 | 2 |
| 325 | 160 | 3 |
| 350 | 180 | 4 |
| 375 | 190 | 5 |
| 400 | 200 | 6 |
| 425 | 220 | 7 |
| 450 | 230 | 8 |
| 475 | 240 | 9 |
| 500 | 260 | 10 |

## Liquid/Dry Measurements

| U.S. | METRIC |
|---|---|
| 1/4 teaspoon | 1.25 milliliters |
| 1/2 teaspoon | 2.5 milliliters |
| 1 teaspoon | 5 milliliters |
| 1 tablespoon (3 teaspoons) | 15 milliliters |
| 1 fluid ounce (2 tablespoons) | 30 milliliters |
| 1/4 cup | 60 milliliters |
| 1/3 cup | 80 milliliters |
| 1/2 cup | 120 milliliters |
| 1 cup | 240 milliliters |
| 1 pint (2 cups) | 480 milliliters |
| 1 quart (4 cups, 32 ounces) | 960 milliliters |
| 1 gallon (4 quarts) | 3.84 liters |
| | |
| 1 ounce (by weight) | 28 grams |
| 1 pound | 448 grams |
| 2.2 pounds | 1 kilogram |

## Lengths

| U.S. | METRIC |
|---|---|
| 1/8 inch | 3 millimeters |
| 1/4 inch | 6 millimeters |
| 1/2 inch | 12 millimeters |
| 1 inch | 2.5 centimeters |